TEACHING
WITH
PURPOSE

How to Thoughtfully Implement
Evidence-Based Practices in Your Classroom

KAREN GAZITH

foreword by Evelyn Lusthaus

Solution Tree | Press

a division of
Solution Tree

555 North Morton Street
Bloomington, IN 47404
800.733.6786 (toll free) / 812.336.7700
FAX: 812.336.7790

email: info@SolutionTree.com
SolutionTree.com

Visit **go.SolutionTree.com/instruction** to download the free reproducibles in this book.

Printed in the United States of America

Library of Congress Cataloging-in-Publication Data

Names: Gazith, Karen, author.
Title: Teaching with purpose : how to thoughtfully implement evidence-based
    practices in your classroom / Karen Gazith.
Description: Bloomington, IN : Solution Tree Press, [2020] | Includes
    bibliographical references and index.
Identifiers: LCCN 2020029112 (print) | LCCN 2020029113 (ebook) | ISBN
    9781951075491 (paperback) | ISBN 9781951075507 (ebook)
Subjects: LCSH: Effective teaching. | Teacher effectiveness. | Classroom
    environment.
Classification: LCC LB1025.3 .G4244 2020 (print) | LCC LB1025.3 (ebook) |
    DDC 371.102--dc23
LC record available at https://lccn.loc.gov/2020029112
LC ebook record available at https://lccn.loc.gov/2020029113

Solution Tree
Jeffrey C. Jones, CEO
Edmund M. Ackerman, President

Solution Tree Press
President and Publisher: Douglas M. Rife
Associate Publisher: Sarah Payne-Mills
Art Director: Rian Anderson
Managing Production Editor: Kendra Slayton
Production Editor: Alissa Voss
Content Development Specialist: Amy Rubenstein
Proofreader: Jessi Finn
Text and Cover Designer: Kelsey Hergül
Editorial Assistants: Sarah Ludwig and Elijah Oates

ACKNOWLEDGMENTS

I would like to thank the many educators whom I have had the great fortune of learning from over the years. I hope to continue to learn from you in the future.

In addition, I would like to thank my editor, Shari Reinhart, as well as Amy Rubenstein and Alissa Voss from Solution Tree. Your assistance and insights were invaluable both in the organization of the manuscript and in the editing.

My husband, Tsafrir, has been a great support throughout the entire process. His reading of the manuscript and keen eye helped to ensure that my message was communicated consistently throughout the book. My children, Ben, Adam, and Adina, and my entire family are wonderful supporters of the work that I do. Finally, I would like to dedicate this book in memory of my mother, Dena Cohen. She was my role model as an educator and set the path for me to continue her journey. She instilled in me a sense of justice and compassion for everyone, but above all, for the most vulnerable.

Solution Tree Press would like to thank the following reviewers:

Kimberly De La Cruz
Director of Secondary
   Teaching and Learning
Westside Community Schools
Omaha, Nebraska

Nicholas A. Emmanuele
English Teacher and
   Department Chair
McDowell Intermediate
   High School
Erie, Pennsylvania

Visit **go.SolutionTree.com/instruction** to
download the free reproducibles in this book.

TABLE OF CONTENTS

Reproducible pages are in italics.

2. Establishing and Communicating Learning Goals 25

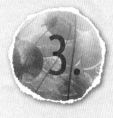

3. Incorporating Strategic Teaching and Learning . . . 43

4. Improving Classroom Management 67

5. Conducting Regular Formative Assessment 89

6. Employing Differentiated Instruction for All Students 109

7. Developing Grit and Perseverance in Yourself and in Your Students 151

ABOUT THE AUTHOR

Karen Gazith, PhD, serves as dean of academics at Les Écoles Talmud Torah Elementary and Herzliah High School. She is also a faculty lecturer in the Department of Educational and Counselling Psychology at McGill University, where she has taught since 1993. She began her teaching career at the Feuerstein Institute in Jerusalem, where she implemented Dr. Feuerstein's Instrumental Enrichment program with young children and adolescents. Since then, she has served as the coordinator of special education in an elementary and high school, and as the director of education for a consortium of schools. She has also taught at Hebrew College in Boston and the University of New Brunswick.

Dr. Gazith holds a strong belief that teachers play a critical role in the success of their students. Over the years, she has presented in Canada, the United States, England, Israel, and Australia on topics related to developing key competencies in leadership and meeting diverse needs in the classroom, assessment, and instruction.

Dr. Gazith has won numerous awards of excellence at Federation CJA in Montreal, including the Pearl Feintuch Award, the Gewurz Award for Jewish Educational Leadership, and Federation CJA awards of excellence. She was also awarded scholarships from Les Fonds pour la Formation de chercheurs et l'aide à la recherche from the Quebec government and from the Scottish Rite Foundation for doctoral research. Dr. Gazith holds a doctorate in educational psychology from McGill University.

Visit Dr. Gazith's website, teachingmeanslearning.com, to learn more about her work.

To book Dr. Gazith for professional development, contact pd@SolutionTree.com.

FOREWORD

There are few people more passionate about teaching and learning than Karen Gazith. She has spent her career laser-focused on how students can succeed in school, both by studying the field of effective teacher-learning practices and by immersing herself in classrooms to put these practices into play. Dr. Gazith has been guiding teachers and educational leaders to use principles and strategies that have been proven effective through more than forty years of rigorous educational research. She has mentored beginning teachers as well as experienced, proficient teachers to become more skilled in employing effective, research-based strategies that can reach every student in the diverse, multi-ability classrooms of today. Her mission: assist teachers to teach more effectively so that their students will learn more successfully.

In this practical, user-friendly book, Dr. Gazith asks, Why not use the practices that have been shown beyond doubt to be effective? She identifies seven of the most outstanding evidence-based practices that can be used at any stage, from preK to university; for any subject or topic; for any student at any level of competence and ability. Each practice has its own chapter in which she provides a clear explanation, research that has shown it to be effective, examples from real classrooms, step-by-step strategies for how to implement it, worksheets with summaries, further examples, and planning activities. Her thesis: that all students, no matter their strengths, weaknesses, gifts, difficulties, talents, or troubles, can learn more easily and with more motivation, interest, confidence, and success when these practices are mastered and employed by teachers.

Teaching With Purpose can be used by individual teachers who master the practices, utilize them with the students, and watch their students grow. It also could serve as the curriculum of a schoolwide or districtwide set of sessions on improving teaching and learning. What a privilege to pursue each practice with others, go back to the classroom to apply them, then return to discuss and analyze the results. It would also be an outstanding text in college programs preparing future teachers; rather than individual professors' favorite ideas about what is good teaching, they would be receiving crucial information about what has been proven.

Teaching With Purpose is a must-read for educators at any and every level in the school system. Enjoy it; use it; benefit from it! Most important, see your students learn and succeed.

Dr. Evelyn Lusthaus
McGill University

INTRODUCTION

Teaching in today's climate is not easy. There are a host of expectations placed on teachers to support the socio-emotional needs of each child and at the same time meet ministry or state expectations. All of this can be very demanding, within an environment that is increasingly diverse academically as well as behaviorally. While you always intend to bring your best self to the classroom, knowing your students are watching and learning from you, there are times you feel overwhelmed by a system that sets greater-than-ever-before demands on you. You are sensitive to the fact that every student is a unique individual, and you want to consistently provide each one with equal opportunities. You want your students to learn at their potential, notwithstanding their individual limited or expansive capabilities and regardless of class, gender, or race, but sometimes you feel that the demands that are being placed on you are beyond what any teacher should be expected to do. Teaching state or ministry standards with an expectation that a very diverse student body will succeed is overwhelming. But what seems most unfair is what is oftentimes expressed by teachers—that the expectations placed on them are not matched with supports enabling them to reach these lofty goals. Teachers can be held to high standards in terms of ensuring students' academic success, but in order to achieve this, the *how* is often lacking.

Within the school system, and specifically the classroom, it is possible to meet the ever-changing demands that your school, school board, or state places upon you while still being the change you want to be in the lives of your students, although it is not and never will be easy. Managing a classroom while trying to meet the needs of a diverse student population is often a challenge that teachers face on a daily basis (Baker, 2005; Marzano & Marzano, 2001; O'Hara & Pritchard, 2008). However, your influence has the power to effect real change for your students, leading them to realize their unique gifts and succeed in life both during and after school. It is truly possible for you, as a teacher, to be the face of change in your students' lives.

The impetus for writing this book is to bring constructive, realistic hope to teachers that they can help students find the success that has always been within students' reach. Crucial to keep in mind is the importance of the growth mindset. Students who believe that success is within their reach, and that with extended effort they have the potential to succeed, will have a far more likely chance of succeeding in school. By using specific strategies to implement some basic, yet highly effective, evidence-based best practices, educators and students will experience substantive growth (Dunlosky, Rawson, Marsh, Nathan, & Willingham, 2013; Marzano & Marzano, 2001). My goal in writing this book is to share with you, the educator, evidence-based principles that can serve as best practices in the classroom.

CHANGE BEGINS WITH YOUR BELIEFS

The change begins with your view of student potential. Some take the stance that intelligence is *fixed*—something that's unchangeable and characteristic—and others believe it is *malleable*—something that can be changed (Dweck, 2007). When it comes to education, how you view the malleability of intelligence matters greatly. If you believe that a student who is having difficulty mastering a concept today—for example, understanding how to turn a fraction into a decimal—can master this concept with your guidance and the implementation of effective strategies, then, in essence, you believe that intelligence is malleable. The message you are sending to your students is that learning can take place with effective instruction and an environment conducive to learning. This belief is essential to student success. Your belief in the student leads to students' ability to believe in themselves (Dweck, 2007; Ilhan-Beyaztas & Dawson, 2017).

I began my educational career in 1983 working as an educator at Professor Reuven Feuerstein's Institute of Cognitive Modifiability. Professor Feuerstein, a student of Jean Piaget and Carl Jung, believed that intelligence was malleable and modifiable—certainly not fixed. Professor Feuerstein, who was not alone in these conclusions, held the role of the educator in very high esteem. The educator was the adult in the student's life who served as the expert scaffolder, helping the student make sense of his or her environment and thus enabling the student to respond adaptively (van de Pol, Volman, & Beishuizen, 2010). When students were taught that they could improve, they were able to see intelligence as increasing with effort and hard work.

These students typically had more positive attitudes, a greater appreciation for academic tasks, and stronger learning goals (Blackwell, Rodriguez, & Guerra-Carrillo, 2014; Marzano & Marzano, 2001). In addition, students who felt they belonged in their school, were included by their peers, and had a connection with their teacher or at least one other caring adult were more likely to succeed (Kiefer, Alley, & Ellerbrock, 2015). Students who did not succeed, on the other hand, did not fail because they had an intellectual impairment but rather because their educational environment was lacking stimulation, which prevented the students from reaching their full potential (Bucholz & Sheffler, 2009; Marzano & Marzano, 2001).

Although I only taught at the Institute of Cognitive Modifiability for one year, Professor Feurstein's educational philosophy had a significant impact on my belief in the capacity of the learner and the extremely important role of the educator. These concepts—the malleability of intelligence and the indispensable role of the educator—laid the foundation for my educational belief system. Additionally, over the past thirty-five years, in the various roles I have held, I have observed hundreds of teachers. I've seen excellent teachers at work. I've witnessed their struggles, their triumphs, and everything in between. My years of experience in education have led me to the realization that there are many effective strategies that, when applied on a consistent basis, result in impressive student growth, both because of the effective teaching and learning that is taking place and, equally important, because of the classroom environment that the teacher creates. At times it's intangible, but when I'm in the midst of a rigorous and nurturing classroom environment, I can see that great things are happening. Ultimately, I have found, it's the skill set that you bring to the classroom, your belief system, and your capacity to guide the learning that ultimately unleash the learning potential of your students.

ABOUT THIS BOOK

I know teachers are committed to growth, and I've seen growth in action. Often, when teachers implement new strategies, they subsequently adopt new ways of teaching and shift their views around student capability and success. This usually greatly benefits the students. Classroom management becomes less of a challenge, and learning for all students will be evident. After all, it is the success of the most challenged students that brings the greatest reward.

Up until the past decade, educational research was limited in its scope and usefulness. Classroom environments are not optimal research labs because of the number of variables that are difficult, if not impossible, to control, most notably teachers' level of expertise and student academic diversity (Connolly, 2009). A further obstacle is the chasm that exists between the ivory tower (that is, the research) and the trenches (the classrooms). Important educational research exists, but for decades it has been out of the hands of those who need it most—the teachers—either because it was in a language that didn't seem to fit the reality of the classroom environment or because it was written in research journals that most teachers don't have access to (Drill, Miller, & Behrstock-Sherratt, 2012). Today, however, we are living through somewhat of a renaissance in the field of educational research. The work of researchers such as Robert Marzano, John Hattie, and David Sousa, referenced in this book, has brought educational research to the educator in a form that is clear and implementable. Furthermore, the field of neuroscience offers great hope for educators. It's only in its embryonic stage, but current research in this field nevertheless offers educators much new information.

As researchers gain greater knowledge about how students learn, teachers can apply this research as practical strategies within their classrooms. However, educators must begin with the belief that all students can succeed. After all, if the adult in the students' life, the person who is supposed to be that expert scaffolder, doesn't believe in students' success, neither will they (Kiefer et al., 2015). Students need their educators to believe, often despite all odds and at all costs, that they will exceed the expectations that everyone holds of them.

In this book, I will focus on evidence-based strategies to support student learning. I have chosen to incorporate seven evidence-based principles of teaching and learning that educational researchers have shown to lead to significant student growth in learning for all students. I have tried to include those principles that have been heavily researched and that I have found to be very effective in the classroom. Ultimately, these seven principles encapsulate my overall vision for education, which has developed over the years as a result of having had the opportunity to work alongside inspiring educators and educational leaders, having spent over ten thousand hours observing teachers, and, finally, having read the plethora of research on evidence-based teaching. *Teaching With Purpose: How to Thoughtfully Implement Evidence-Based Practices in Your Classroom* is divided into seven chapters, each chapter highlighting one of these seven principles. (See figure I.1.)

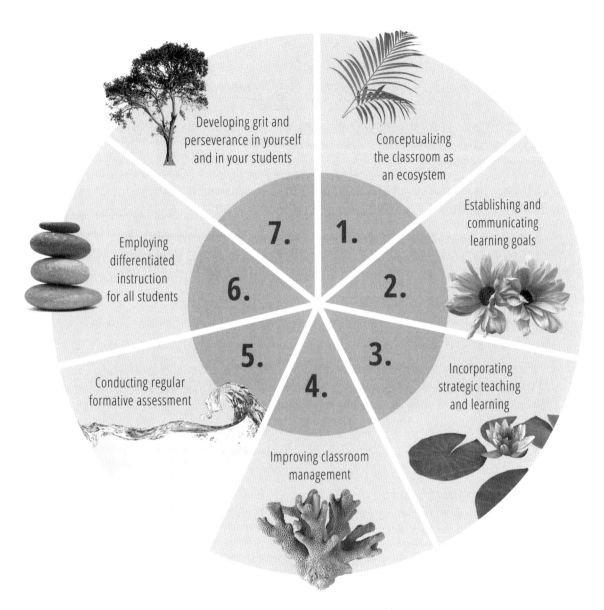

Figure I.1: Seven evidence-based principles for teaching and learning.

The first evidence-based principle I discuss is *conceptualizing the classroom as an ecosystem*. Classrooms are replete with students with varying degrees of readiness. Each time educators interact with students—both those who struggle and those who excel—we are role modeling for all students. In chapter 1, I set a foundation for creating a classroom of equals, in the hopes that students will build these types of welcoming environments both while they are in school and when they reach adulthood.

Chapter 2 addresses the second principle, *establishing and communicating learning goals*. This principle uses the structure of what students need to *know*, *understand*, and be able to *do* by the end of each lesson.

In chapter 3, I present the principle of *incorporating strategic teaching and learning*. To show how strategic teaching leads to strategic learning, I introduce the evidence-based concept of modeling ("I do, we do, you do one, you do many") and provide specific examples of how this can be implemented within the classroom.

In chapter 4, I discuss *improving classroom management*. I will detail specific strategies for how to manage a classroom, including the strategy of 4:1, which addresses the ratio of positive to negative feedback in facilitating effective management.

Chapter 5 presents the concept of *conducting regular formative assessment*. In this chapter, I explain the importance of formative assessment as well as very specific hands-on strategies that can be applied during and at the end of every lesson.

In chapter 6, I present the principle of *employing differentiated instruction for all students* and provide specific hands-on strategies that can facilitate student success, such as tic-tac-toe and 2-5-8.

Finally, the last principle, presented in chapter 7, highlights a critical asset, that of *developing grit and perseverance in yourself and in your students*. I hope to help you move students from laziness or apathy toward a more useful paradigm that involves strategies to enable them to keep going in the face of challenges.

Each chapter contains anecdotes from my own teaching and observing experience that exemplify the principles in question. I also provide strategies for implementing the principles in your practice (summarized in a table at the end of each chapter) and give you some next steps at the end of each chapter to help you begin this important work.

Throughout the book, I will be referring to the title, *Teaching With Purpose: How to Thoughtfully Implement Evidence-Based Practices in Your Classroom*, as it is the overarching theme of this book. You are the most important agent in the life of the student and his or her academic success second only to parents. In order for us, as educators, to gain maximum benefit from these strategies, we need to be mindful and purposeful in our planning and every time we enter the classroom. We need to consistently ask ourselves questions such as, How is the student's behavior a sign of an unmet need? How can I respond to students' needs so that they don't need to misbehave to have their needs met? What is my goal for my students in today's lesson? What do I want my students to be able to do by the end of the lesson? What is the most effective way to teach them so that they learn? What is the purpose of this information? How do I share this purpose with my students so that the learning is meaningful for them? And most important of all, How do I leave my voice behind in my students so that they can use that voice in perpetuity to guide them through a procedure, so that they will eventually become successful, independent learners? With the implementation of the seven principles presented in this book, all of these questions will be addressed.

It is important to avoid the misconception that teachers who struggle in the classroom are, more often than not, novices. In my observational experience, both veteran teachers and new teachers struggle in the classroom on occasion, and as a result, the quality of their students' education suffers. This concept will be addressed throughout the book. This struggle could be due to speaking for too long and subsequently losing students' attention, allowing excessive noise and chaos in the classroom and thus creating a learning environment antithetical to student learning, or any number of other things. The good news is this struggle does not have to be the end of the story. Any teacher at any stage of teaching has the power to turn things around and begin leading his or her students toward academic growth.

Therefore, I wrote this book to appeal to teachers new to the field as well as teachers who have more experience teaching yet may be experiencing some challenges. It was also written for the more experienced teachers who are adept at many of the principles that form the foundation of this book but may benefit from incorporating into their teaching practice one or more of the principles that may be present but could be sharpened.

Teachers new to the field of teaching may benefit from reading one chapter at a time, learning about the principle and the evidence that supports its implementation. It would also be useful to use just of few of the strategies included in each chapter to put the principle into practice. More experienced teachers who may be having difficulty in one or more of the areas presented here could go right to the chapter that focuses on the problem area and hopefully benefit from some of the strategies included in that particular chapter. Finally, the more experienced teachers may want to add a few new strategies to their repertoire in a particular area such as establishing clearer learning goals, or learning new ways to assess whether or not students have mastered these goals. However you intend to use this book, the strategies and principles contained within will help all teachers improve their practice and increase students' chances of success both inside and outside the classroom.

1

Conceptualizing the Classroom as an Ecosystem

How a teacher views the potential for success of each and every student is of optimal importance in terms of how students come to view themselves and one another. Ultimately, we aim to create classroom environments that model the type of society we all hope to be part of: one in which each human being is valued for his or her contribution rather than a society where value is placed on those who are perceived as being more successful—and where a school's success is often viewed in terms of student grades. Effective teachers have a common trait—they see the value in all students—and therefore students come to see their own value as well as the value of their classmates.

This chapter begins by explaining some challenges you may have seen in your classroom—many of these situations will be familiar to you, as either a new or a veteran teacher—before describing the principle of *conceptualizing the classroom as an ecosystem* and describing the research and evidence surrounding this practice. It then describes several strategies you can use as you begin applying this principle in your classroom to help address the aforementioned challenge. The chapter concludes with a plan for next steps to take over the coming months.

⚡ THE CHALLENGE

When entering a classroom, it becomes immediately apparent to me if the environment is one of equity—in which each student is valued regardless of his or her academic success or struggles—or if students who struggle are perceived as less valuable. At times this is obvious because it is immediately stated as I enter the classroom. A teacher may whisper with hand signals indicating that certain students in the classroom "are weak" or "struggle" or "are unlikely to pass the year." Despite the whispering, I often wonder if the target students pick up the message from the hand signals indicating lack of success or failure. After I have spent a few minutes in the classroom, the division between the students who struggle and those who succeed is apparent as well. Those who are successful seem more engaged, talk more in class, and look happier. The students who struggle often appear disengaged, quieter, or as though they are looking for any opportunity to leave the class.

In contrast, a classroom built on equity, whereby each student is valued, is equally palpable upon entry into the classroom. The environment feels welcoming, and a division between those who are academically successful and those who are not is indiscernible. Students are all equally engaged and seem to want to be present in the classroom.

From my years observing classrooms, what seems so important to the overall success of students is the way in which teachers view all students and whether or not teachers believe that all students are capable of academic success. In this chapter, specific strategies to create an environment—an ecosystem—that brings out the capacity of all students will be addressed.

🌱 THE PRINCIPLE

This challenge can be solved by viewing each classroom within the greater school community as a place where participants (the students and teacher) and their physical learning space interact in an ecosystem that values all members. One dictionary definition of *ecosystem* (*Oxford English Dictionary*, n.d.) is "a biological community of interacting organisms and their physical environment." To apply this definition to schools—considering an ecosystem as simply a community, instead of a biological community—each school is an ecosystem, and each classroom is an ecosystem within the larger one. If we believe that a school is an ecosystem, instead of a set of isolated, unconnected rooms, it has tremendous implications for how we organize schools and classrooms and conduct ourselves within them. All students, but especially those who are academically or socially vulnerable, are highly influenced by the environment within which they are learning. When you view student success not only as an individual accomplishment, but also in terms of a holistic set of parts, you can begin to focus on all of the different parts within that environment. How students are perceived by their teacher, their classmates, students in other grades, and the administration will have an impact on how they view themselves. Students see themselves in our eyes. If we care for their inner souls, we will be focusing on how they interact with one another, how we group them for assignments so that students are not left without a partner, how we introduce them to new material so that they feel capable as learners and not hopeless—and all of this with a belief that success is a requirement for all and not an option for some.

The concept of individual classrooms functioning as ecosystems primarily refers to how the students within them are perceived by their teachers and their classmates and how the classroom environment is structured to ensure that a community of learners is created—and as a result, how the teachers, students, and administrators interact and influence one another. Ultimately, your goal should be equity of opportunity for all within that ecosystem.

To understand the interactions that exist in classrooms, and to look with a skeptical eye at whether students within them truly have equal opportunity to thrive, it is important to examine how the field of education has transformed itself since the 1950s, specifically considering the integration and inclusion of special education students.

Until the 1960s, special education and regular education formed separate worlds, and little interaction existed between them. If a student was identified as having a special educational need at any point during his or her education, he or she was placed either in a special class within a regular school or, more commonly, in a separate school for special education (Katsiyannis, Yell, & Bradley, 2001; Martin, Martin, & Terman, 1996; Salend & Garrick Duhaney, 2011; U.S. Department of Education, 2010).

In 1975, the U.S. federal government passed Public Law 94-142, the *Education for All Handicapped Children Act*, which stated that children with physical disabilities were entitled to an education in the least restrictive environment (LRE; U.S. Department of Education, 1975). This was laudable, but to a great extent, the ambiguity of the statement "least restrictive environment" was problematic and left to interpretation of the reader. Some believed it referred to students spending the majority of their day within the regular classroom. Others believed it was sufficient that they were included within the school environment but spent a significant portion of the day in special classes within the regular school. Over the course of time, students with handicaps and disabilities were mainstreamed into regular classes (Rueda, Gallego, & Moll, 2000; Salend & Garrick Duhaney, 2011).

Researchers and educators used the term *mainstreaming* for this process because of its societal context. Inherent in the concept of mainstreaming is the assumption that there is a code of behavior that the majority of people in a society adopt. It presupposes that those who enter the mainstreamed society—or, for the sake of this conversation, the classroom environment—have either been socialized to exhibit these behaviors or been properly taught to adopt them (Kavale, 2010). From an educational perspective, the assumption was that students with mild handicaps would learn adaptive behaviors by being placed in a regular classroom (Kavale, 2010; Reynolds, Wang, & Walberg, 1987). However, a lack of focus on accommodations needed to include students with handicaps meant mainstreaming as a concept lost ground. Initially, as students with special needs were being mainstreamed into regular classrooms, school leadership gave attention to the academic, behavioral, and social skills that the students needed to possess in order to succeed in regular classrooms. Oftentimes, students would learn these essential skills in special or remedial classes in the hope that they'd be able to transfer them within the classroom (Anderson-Inman, Walker, & Purcell, 1984; Fuchs & Fuchs, 1994). The question for leaders to ask was, "What does the student need to possess?" rather than "What environment must the teacher create?" (Ball & Cohen, 1996; Fuchs & Fuchs, 1994; Tonelson, 1981).

The lofty expectation that students would be taught behaviors that would enable them to fit in with the mainstream was unrealistic and untenable for many students, and it placed a new and unfamiliar burden on teachers (Scruggs & Mastropieri, 1996). Theoretically, the idea was a good one—the recognition that within any classroom, as within any society, there are different groups that maintain their own uniqueness while also developing behaviors that are necessary to function as a whole. However, as with integration, classroom teachers themselves made few changes to instruction, curriculum, and classroom environment. Studies exploring teacher perceptions about inclusion identified various issues regarding training, class size, specialized support, and time that made the difference between feeling successful and feeling unsuccessful with inclusion (Smith & Smith, 2000).

As the field of special education continued to advance and an increasing number of students with labels such as *learning disability, attention deficit hyperactivity disorder*, and *mild intellectual handicap* were being educated in regular classrooms, there was a need to create new styles of teaching. Researchers began examining ways in which students with diverse learning needs could be included in classrooms, as teachers struggled to adjust their teaching styles to include all students (McIntosh, Vaughn, Schumm, Haager, & Lee, 1994; Tomlinson et al., 2003). This struggle continues as teachers seek to enhance their repertoire of teaching strategies to include the vast diversity of student ability within the classroom. It is essential here to keep two things in mind. First, students with academic challenges need to have those challenges addressed with effective teaching practices. Yet at the same time, it is essential that, despite these challenges that exist and will continue to exist, teachers create an environment whereby all students feel valued and capable as learners.

My experience over the years has led me to believe that while school systems have made efforts to educate students across the continuum of academic, social, and behavioral needs, they have placed far less of an emphasis on ensuring that, within the classroom environment, those who struggle are not made to feel less valued than their more academically successful classmates. While academic success is important, equal importance should be placed on how we need to interact with one another so that each member feels valued for what he or she brings to the classroom.

🌐 THE STRATEGY

When conceptualizing the classroom as an ecosystem, consider one or more of the following strategies.

- Ensure students are intellectually, emotionally, and physically safe to learn.

- Appreciate all students.

- Foster a growth mindset.

- Replace the one-size-fits-all approach to teaching and learning with facilitation of learning.

- Model the behavior you want your students to follow.

Ensure Students Are Intellectually, Emotionally, and Physically Safe to Learn

The classroom ecosystem has a life force of its own whereby a sequential, coherent curriculum is not enough for genuine learning to occur. Rather, learning is only possible when students feel intellectually, emotionally, and physically safe and supported (Holley & Steiner, 2005). Maslow's (1943) hierarchy of human needs explains that learning can only take place when learners' basic needs of safety are met and learning becomes a priority. Furthermore, the way students emotionally see the world sets the foundation for learning (Yahaya, 2014). Research indicates that students report being more likely to learn about others, expand their own viewpoints, increase their self-awareness, and develop effective communication skills in environments they feel safe in (Holley & Steiner, 2005). As the teacher, you must consider your students' personal development and well-being as well as their academic achievement and provide them with a sustainable environment in which to thrive wholly.

The classroom setting should be a comfortable, stimulating physical space that is conducive to growth and learning, celebrates diversity, and offers equity of opportunity (Holley & Steiner, 2005; Murphy & Hallinger, 2006; Skiba & Rausch, 2013). This will be explained in great detail in chapter 6 (page 109).

Appreciate All Students

Every student-teacher relationship is different, and on any given day, the dynamics and expectations between you and your students will vary. Your understanding of and tolerance for so-called misbehavior will also differ from that of other teachers. You might see an active student as exuberant and joyful, while another teacher might describe the same student as hyperactive and disruptive. Strive to always see the best in your students and appreciate their unique gifts. Students, especially those in the younger grades, are highly influenced by how you view them and their classmates (Furrer, Skinner, & Pitzer, 2014). What they hear being said is not lost on any of them, and the most sensitive and struggling students are the ones who tend to be the most attuned to your opinion of them. Being the kind of teacher who can bring a mindful appreciation and even celebration of your students' differences—and the kind of teacher who, above all, models genuine acceptance of all students—creates a safe and nurturing environment where all students are allowed to thrive (Bucholz & Sheffler, 2009). Genuine acceptance cannot be superficial but must be felt deeply, because students are astute and sophisticated observers.

Foster a Growth Mindset

The traditional notion of the classroom—that students are either "with [intelligence] or without it" (Erickson, 1996b)—represents the antithesis of an ecosystem that values each of its members. Rather than being limited by the traditional notion that *success* refers to strong academic aptitude and social status, students and teachers should instead have a broad conception of what strengths are and a clear understanding that although these strengths and weaknesses may be different from student to student, each person is capable of building on and improving his or her abilities. For example, a strength might be a student's performance art or music capacity or knowledge in a particular subject, even if that subject doesn't directly pertain to a subject covered as part of the curriculum (such as dinosaurs or Walt Disney movies).

To that end, Stanford University professor of psychology Carol Dweck's seminal research on the psychological mindset has contributed significantly. According to Dweck (2006), when people have a *fixed mindset*, they believe basic qualities like intelligence or talent are innate, fixed traits. Individuals with a *growth mindset*, however, believe talent can be developed through hard work, good strategies, and input from others (Dweck, 2006). When you, the educator, place emphasis on creating an environment that instills a growth mindset approach to learning, you impress on your students that they are capable of improving. You impress them with an "I can do it" attitude, instilling in them the understanding that success can be theirs when effort, perseverance, and hard work are applied. With that, their confidence soars. Your responsibility is then to provide effective, explicit instruction in the acquisition of skills, and to also model a growth mindset in your own behavior. A growth mindset approach has a far greater likelihood to nurture the seeds of successful learning and achievement in a student than a fixed mindset (Dweck, 2006). When students believed that they had the capacity to succeed, that it was within their control, and when they were explained the science of success from a brain-based perspective, there was an increase in their motivation as well as their actual performance.

Replace the One-Size-Fits-All Approach to Teaching With Facilitation of Learning

With integration, as well as with mainstreaming, general education teachers were faced with teaching an increased number of students with increasingly diverse needs, armed with only a few changes to instruction, curriculum, and classroom environment to prepare them. As a result, educators were not seeing the type of success they were hoping to see as a result of this integration. Additionally, a heavy burden was placed on teachers to provide differentiated strategies to this diverse student population (Simpson, 1997). This one-size-fits-all educational model, with the teacher acting primarily as the deliverer of information, needed to be replaced with a new model of teaching, one where the teacher is instead the facilitator of learning (Biggs, 1999).

Schools need to develop a framework for you, the teacher, that begins with an early intervention model of assessment of basic skills and is followed by a series of instructional tools that are effective for the diversity that exists. Yet, for this to happen, schools need to examine the ecosystem that is the classroom.

Model the Behavior You Want Your Students to Follow

The behavior and the life experiences teachers bring into the classroom contribute to shaping their students (Blackwell et al., 2014; Kiefer et al., 2015; Marzano & Marzano, 2001; van de Pol et al., 2010). We are their examples. Students don't just learn from us what we teach—they also learn who we are, and so it makes sense to consistently model the same behaviors that we ask of our students. This modeling gives students more reason to trust us. It pays off when you can stop yourself from raising your voice while you're also asking them to be quiet or from acting disappointed in them while also insisting that they not give up trying.

Theodore Sizer and Nancy Faust Sizer remind us in their book *The Students Are Watching: Schools and the Moral Contract* (2000) that everything we say and do as educators becomes a life lesson for our students. We become powerful role models when we practice honest and ethical behavior, and we fail our students when we don't.

Perhaps the most compelling lesson for our students, and often the most hypocritical practice of many schools, is when educators ask students to include everyone, yet we don't do the same ourselves. For example, we categorize them (and allow them to categorize each other) when we require team captains to choose their teams in physical education. Inevitably, the poorest in sports are left standing at the end. Likewise, we spend hours explaining the consequences of leaving students out, not including others in recess activities, and not inviting others to play, yet we frequently sort students according to ability in our classrooms. Those deemed strong students end up in the high-level groups, and those who struggle end up in the low-level streams. Why is it that we allow certain students into advanced courses but not others? When students who do not possess the prerequisite skills to master more challenging content want to give it a try and we withhold such opportunity from them, they receive a message that says opportunities for advancement are not for them (Martin, 2013; Phillips, 2008).

TEACHING BY EXAMPLE

It's incumbent on us to remember that our students are always watching us and learning from our actions—often far more than they learn from our words. Many years ago, I had a student in one of my graduate classes who required considerable attention from the teacher. She was the first one to arrive in class and the last to leave. During class, she would impulsively call out answers that were often inaccurate, incorrect, or unrelated to the topic of the day. She worried that there wouldn't be enough copies of the handouts (before online portals were popular) even though there were always extras, and she would anxiously come up to the front of the class and plead for a copy before they were circulated. Students who were paired with her during classwork remarked on her inability to respect physical space. Each time she engaged in challenging behavior of some form, I noticed thirty-five sets of eyes on me. This was a class on inclusive education, and the students were studying my interactions with her to see how I responded to a student with challenging needs. I knew that each time I interacted with her, they were watching, and I was teaching them an important lesson—perhaps one even more important than the course content.

I made sure to respond with patience, even though in all honesty, it wasn't always easy. I would give her a copy of the handout before the others, if for no other reason than because she needed to have one in hand so that she could relax and listen to the instructions. If she didn't receive one in advance, the extra few moments of anticipation waiting to receive her copy weren't good either for her or for the other students in the class. I also tried to spend a few minutes speaking with her before class began. She needed me to know certain things about how her week had transpired, and these few moments I spent listening to her seemed to help her relax later in the lesson and focus on the classwork. The message I hoped to transmit to the students through my actions was that her needs were clear and obvious to both me and the others, and they needed to be met. I didn't see any of it as unfair because she had needs that the others didn't seem to have. During group work, I expected them to include her and work with her just as I had modeled. It wasn't always easy for me to model this behavior, but it absolutely made a difference.

What is most interesting and disturbing is to listen to the way students interact with the so-called troublemakers in their classes. Maybe this has happened to you or a colleague of yours: a teacher repeatedly scolds a student who is struggling with a basic instruction such as "Take out your books," "Stop talking," or "Clean up the papers around your desk." Soon, the other students begin uttering similar comments to this student. They are simply imitating what they hear, and they are inclined to think, "Well, if the teacher can talk that way, then why can't I?" We've all seen this happen, even though it is never a teacher's intention.

It's difficult to discern the difference between allowing students to move as needed and accepting what should be deemed unacceptable behavior. This comes with experience and a lot of time spent in reflection. But a good rule of thumb is to figure out whether it helps the student learn or detracts from his or her learning. If a student learns best standing on one foot at the back of the class, and it doesn't detract from the learning of others, it should be permitted. The lesson of acceptance, tolerance, and thinking in terms of the best interest of students will be conveyed to all. My experience has shown me that when we say to students, "I am giving you this special privilege and I know you won't take advantage of it," they never do.

The classroom structure and acceptance of differences we model will ultimately impact the way students manage themselves. An open and fluid structure that tolerates movement and student interaction will lead to fewer students being perceived as weak, inept, or incompetent (Dunbar, 2004). As Erickson (1996b) said so insightfully, "It (learning) is a risky business" (p. 99). Classroom rules are necessary elements of any well-managed classroom, but too many of them can be oppressive, especially for those who have difficulty with imposed structure. The structure of the classroom and the openness of the teacher to difference will determine how the students view one another (Dunbar, 2004). Classrooms can be "sites for risk, respect and trust" (Erickson, 1996b, p. 99), or they can be dangerous and potentially humiliating places.

Teaching can't be merely about academic standards and behavioral expectations. Each class must exemplify the ecosystem that you hope to create. That ecosystem will always be idiosyncratic because it will represent your uniqueness and how you choose to structure your class, but hopefully it will be a safe haven for students and a place where each student is judged by his or her own merit instead of being merely a data point on a continuum—better than some and worse than others. As the leader of the pack, you can set the tone for learning and have great influence on how students perceive themselves and others (Furrer et al., 2014; Rasmussen, 1998).

GIVING STUDENTS A SECOND CHANCE TO SUCCEED

I once witnessed a wonderful example of modeling in a sixth-grade mathematics class. The teacher was working through a problem on the board, periodically stopping and asking students to complete parts of the calculations using their calculators. One student was asked to provide a response. It was incorrect. The student appeared embarrassed, tilted her head to one side, and looked as though she was about to cry. The other students were completely silent. I held my breath, hoping that she would get another opportunity to respond. This could be a make-it-or-break-it moment for this student, leaving her with a sense of either competence or incompetence.

Fortunately, the teacher asked another student to define a word in the problem that might have been misunderstood by this student, and then gave her another chance to respond—and this time she answered correctly. The other students smiled, visibly pleased that she got it right. This was a lesson for this student—don't give up; you'll get a second chance. As per the growth mindset, when students expend the effort, positive results ensue—in other words, it's not hopeless. The lesson was no less important for the other students: give people a second chance and revel in their success.

Create the type of classroom that highlights the weak versus the strong, and there will be a tangible division between those perceived as capable and those perceived as weak and inept (Freire, 1970). In a study on teachers' beliefs about transformability, the authors recalled the limiting of opportunities and other injustices because of ability labels. These experiences helped them understand the injustice inherent in treating differences in learners and their learning as a reflection of differences in individual intellectual potential (Hart, Dixon, Drummond, & McIntyre, 2004). When, on the other hand, you bring with you an added overall awareness into the classroom, you create a well-nourished environment—one that recognizes that within the ecosystem of your classroom, everyone needs each other to thrive—and the system will adjust itself to meet the diverse needs of its inhabitants.

The strategies listed in this section—ensure students are intellectually, emotionally, and physically safe to learn; appreciate all students; foster a growth mindset; replace the one-size-fits-all approach to teaching with facilitation of learning; and model the behavior you want your students to follow—feed what is necessary for the classroom ecosystem to thrive so that students feel safe and ready to learn. As discussed previously, the environment within which students are learning has a great impact on their potential and their success.

To begin implementing these ideas, you can choose from some of the strategies listed in the "Strategies for Creating a Supportive Classroom Ecosystem" reproducible on page 21, or print your own blank version of this chart at **go.SolutionTree.com/instruction** and jot down some of your own ideas.

⌐ NEXT STEPS

Think about how you can incorporate one new strategy each month, and record your ideas in the reproducible "Template for New Strategies to Incorporate Each Month" found on page 23). Have your students view you as a learner along with them. Share with them how you are working on creating a safe environment for all as you bring these strategies into the classroom. Have a celebration each month for the wonderful classroom ecosystem that you are all a part of creating.

Strategies for Creating a Supportive Classroom Ecosystem

STRATEGY	ACTION STEPS	EXAMPLE
Ensure students are intellectually, emotionally, and physically safe to learn.	Teach both academic and social-personal development within context.	Teach students academic skills using evidence-based strategies such as *reciprocal teaching* (Palincsar, 1986). The strategies include: predict what the text is going to be about using images and tables; summarize key components of the passage; clarify any words or phrases that are unclear; ask yourself a question about the text; and predict what the next passage is going to be about. Teach students social and personal development, such as how to enter a conversation (look to see if students are standing within close proximity of one another. If so, the conversation is most likely private. If not, walk over, listen to the conversation for a few moments, then ask a question, join in, and add to the conversation).
Appreciate all students.	Get to know students' interests.	Provide students with an interest inventory (a good one is the interest-a-lyzer by Joseph S. Renzulli [1977]). Get to know students' unique interests so that activities in the class can highlight their strengths.
Foster a growth mindset.	Develop a growth mindset in all students.	Focus on what students need to do in order to be successful. Use language such as, What strategies can you use to help you get this done? What is your plan? or What resources can you use to help you reach your goal?

Page 1 of 2

Replace the one-size-fits-all approach to learning.	Incorporate as many opportunities as possible where challenges are presented to students whereby there is no correct answer.	At the end of a unit of study give students pictures of random objects (a dog, a suitcase, a cob of corn), and ask them to make connections between what they just learned and the image. For example, at the end of a unit about the Enlightenment, students could be asked to make a connection between what they just learned and a suitcase. The student might say, "People now felt that they had the ability to go places."
Model the behavior you want your students to follow.	Be a good role model.	Always speak kindly to students, especially those who struggle. Students will likely emulate the way you address all students, especially those who struggle academically or behaviorally and are most in need of positive feedback. Place students in groups that represent diversity. Walk around and provide examples about how to give and receive positive input from group members. Speak kindly to and about other staff members.
Encourage your students.	Encourage risk taking.	Applaud student effort and reinforce students for encouraging one another, both when students experience success and when they don't.

Template for New Strategies to Incorporate Each Month

MONTH	STRATEGY	REFLECTION

Establishing and Communicating Learning Goals

"Begin with the end in mind" is one of the seven habits of highly effective people in Stephen Covey's (1989) best-selling book of the same title. In simple terms, it's about starting out with a clear idea of what you want to gain. This informs the steps you take, so it's always leading you there. It's based on the principle that things are created twice: first, in your mind, and second, in physical reality (Covey, 1989). After all, if you don't know where you are going, how can you ever be sure you will get there?

To begin with the end in mind is a simple yet potent concept that teachers can apply in the classroom much in the same way a performance coach might ask an athlete to train for a big race while imagining placing first at the finish line. Another way to think about this is to compare lesson design to the writing of a film. A film is written scene by scene. The screenwriter begins with a message, and the scenes are developed so that at the film's completion, the intended message will be transmitted to the audience. When lesson and unit goals are clearly and explicitly developed, segment by segment, the lesson—like the film—culminates in the realization of the goals.

When you are sure about the goals that you hope your students will attain, you will find it much easier to plan your lessons efficiently, which will enable you to communicate the lesson's purpose to the students. This, in turn, allows you to accurately measure its efficacy. Not only does this set you up for success, it also provides the students with all the tools they need to perform.

Let's return for a moment to the title and theme of this book: *Teaching With Purpose*. Critical to your success in the classroom is to begin with the end in mind. You should consider the questions, What do I want my students to learn, and what evidence will enable me to see if they've learned it? This concept of beginning with the end in mind, or *backward design*, was brought to the world of education by Jay McTighe and Grant Wiggins and has since become an integral concept in many learning environments effective in meeting the needs of all students (Childe, Sands, & Pope, 2009; Kantorski, Sanford-Dolly, Commisso, & Pollack, 2019; McTighe & Wiggins, 1999; Richards, 2013). They highlighted the critical need to begin with the learning goals that you are hoping to achieve by the end of the lesson or unit. According to these educators, essential to knowing if learning goals are being met is knowing what these goals are. How can you ensure that you avoid having to guess if goals have been met—or discovering later that they have not been met for some students? Through purposeful preparation before the term and ahead of each class time. Planning lessons, collecting and organizing material, and creating timelines are some of the critical steps to take that will help you know with confidence if students have or have not met your intended goals. Just because you taught it does not mean that every student learned it. For students to achieve the successes of which they're capable, it's important to be clear about what you want them to learn, thereby making the articulation of learning goals for each lesson and the communication of goals to students a fundamental principle of effective teaching and learning (Cleary, Morgan, & Marzano, 2017; Marzano & Brown, 2009; McTighe & Wiggins, 1999; Whetten, 2007; Wiggins & McTighe, 1998).

Oftentimes, teachers begin by teaching according to the textbook and then assume that students have learned. However, this very practice must be avoided—we should never assume learning (Ball & Cohen, 1996). With a clear purpose and direction, it's possible to know whether or not students have mastered the goals. When you're clear and well prepared, your students easily know what you expect from them, and this allows them to, each in their own time, start to take responsibility for their own learning. Clearly defined lesson goals help them understand what they're preparing to learn and how they will be assessed. This facilitates their ability to grasp the material and identify the desired outcomes, and also encourages them to effectively develop autonomy (Cleary et al., 2017; Marzano & Marzano, 2001; Seidel, Rimmele, & Prenzel, 2005).

This chapter begins by explaining some obstacles or challenges you may have seen in your classroom where learning goals were not clear before describing the principle of *establishing and communicating learning goals* and describing the research and evidence surrounding this practice. It then describes several strategies you can use as you begin applying this principle in your classroom to help you address the challenge and ensure that all lessons begin with clear and effectively communicated goals. The chapter concludes with a plan for next steps to take over the coming months.

⚡ THE CHALLENGE

Looking back on my own high school experience, I remember that in most classes, there were no set goals; instead, the textbook was the focus of our learning. I remember feeling lost much of the time because I had no sense of what I was expected to do or what I was supposed to know. While many of the teachers let us know what to expect in the first introduction class, they didn't follow up with explicit goals, and they paid little or no attention to whether we were all on track in terms of the learning goals. It was all so confusing, and I felt there was no direction. I remember wondering, "Why am I learning this?" Many of my teachers taught by the book, testing us after a certain number of chapters to assess our learning and marking the tests without giving us any feedback. In contrast, I fondly remember one of my English teachers who was explicit about his expectations from us. He wrote the daily goals on the blackboard, and I remember that guidance alone making all the difference in my own personal approach to learning—because now I knew what was expected of me.

It is difficult to expect students to master knowledge acquisition and skills without yourself having a clear sense of what it is that you want your students to accomplish. Though we often have a tacit sense of our goals, without a clear articulation of what success looks like, it is very challenging if at all possible to create effective lessons that teach students these tacit goals. A further challenge occurs when we may have a sense of what these goals are but do not communicate them to our students. We are evaluating students on the success or failure to accomplish learning goals, and thus they are entitled to know what these goals are at the start of each lesson and unit.

⊕ THE PRINCIPLE

It is important to focus on learning goals in addition to the agenda for the day or the activities for the lesson. While the agenda might be important as a signpost for both you and your students, much like a to-do list, it shouldn't replace the need to communicate learning goals for students. The agenda or activities for the day state what you will be covering, but it does not communicate what the students will need to learn (Wiggins & McTighe, 2007).

In 2009, Robert Marzano, cofounder of Marzano Research and author of over fifty education books and two hundred articles, wrote a book exclusively devoted to designing learning goals. *Designing and Teaching Learning Goals and Objectives* (2009a) summarizes a plethora of research, all confirming the importance of goals to the success of student learning. In particular, he cites eighteen meta-analyses and uses the statistical measure of *effect size* to indicate the effectiveness of the strategy employed by the teacher. Effect size indicates how many standard deviations, either larger or smaller, the average score is for students who were provided with a particular strategy in comparison to the average score for students who did not benefit from the strategy. In all studies, the effect sizes range from 0.42 to 1.37 when teachers communicate learning goals to students, indicating that in every study utilizing lesson goal presentation, average student scores increased by 0.42 to 1.37 standard deviations. To further clarify the importance of lesson goals, an effect size of 0.40 results in a 16-percentile-point gain, and an effect size of 0.5 results in a 19-percentile-point gain (Marzano, 2009a). Therefore, simply put, students do better when teachers begin their lessons with a clear articulation of their learning goals than when goals are not communicated to them.

Marzano (2009a) further examines the effectiveness of learning goals as they pertain specifically to writing. He highlights five specific studies whereby clarity of goals indicating both the purpose and the expectations communicated to students resulted in an effect size of 0.70, or a 26-percentile-point gain (Marzano, 2009a). John Hattie, in his book *Visible Learning for Teachers* (2012), identifies learning goals as having an effect size of 0.68.

In their book *Developing Assessment-Capable Visible Learners, Grades K–12*, Frey, Hattie, and Fisher (2018) highlight the importance of articulating both learning intentions (goals) and success criteria. They use the analogy of a GPS to explain these two concepts. The GPS informs travelers of their final destination, much like the role that learning intentions or goals have in the classroom. Learning goals indicate to students what they need to know, understand, and be able to do by the end of the lesson or unit. The success criteria provide feedback to the travelers as to how close they are to their destination and whether they have taken a wrong turn. This essential facet of teaching and learning is accomplished through ongoing formative assessment, which serves to inform learners of their proximity to the goal and what needs to be adjusted in order to get there. (More detail on formative assessment can be found in chapter 5, page 89.) According to

Fisher and Frey (2018), both learning goals and formative assessment are critical elements of success, with an effect size of 0.75.

According to Chappuis and Stiggins (2002) of the Assessment Training Institute in Ontario, "Students can hit any target they can see that holds still for them" (p. 34). The Ontario Ministry of Education (2010) puts a very significant emphasis on the clear articulation of learning goals, whereby teachers are encouraged to begin each lesson by communicating the goals or targets that students are expected to reach.

It is helpful to the student when teachers are purposeful in their planning in order to contextualize students' learning, and they are asked to design a curriculum that seeks to impart sophisticated and deep understanding (Ontario Ministry of Education, 2010; Wiggins & McTighe, 1998, 2007). However, in order to reach this level of sophisticated comprehension, basic knowledge and skills need to be developed first. The premise is that students should be advised and made aware of what they are expected to get out of the lessons.

Finally, we ask students to monitor their learning trajectory and evaluate if they are on track or if there needs to be a change in their course of action. If students are working through a mathematics problem, for example, they should monitor themselves throughout the process to evaluate if they are on track or if they should employ a different strategy. Inherent to students' ability to monitor the effectiveness of their work is their knowledge of what the goal of the lesson is. Knowing the goal is important toward this process of self-monitoring (Gonzalez & Leticia, 2013).

What is so powerful about this is that the sole clarity of learning goals and the communication of these goals to students result in a significant improvement in student performance (Allen & Tanner, 2006; Chappuis & Stiggins, 2002; Fisher & Frey, 2018; Hattie, 2012; Marzano, 2009a). The type of goal is equally important. Goals that highlight the specific content students are expected to master are more effective than the communication of a specific grade (Marzano, 2009a). For example, students do better if they are told that they're expected to know the elements of an expository text and to produce a text that incorporates all of the elements than if they're told that they are expected to get a score of 80 percent. Knowing this, it would be unfair not to incorporate learning goals into each unit and lesson. Clearly defined learning goals are powerful; they give the students an understanding of what they're learning and why. Lesson goals attach a reason and motivation to help master the overall learning goals (Brophy, 1986; Dean, Hubbell, Pitler, & Stone, 2012).

In establishing learning goals, it's important to begin with curricular standards, competencies, or progression of learnings. Each state or jurisdiction has its own set of standards, competencies, or progressions of learning that inform teachers of the overarching content, skills, procedures, and knowledge that students need to master for each grade level. These standards are not a curriculum, nor do they inform teachers what needs to be done on a daily basis. This is where the learning goals come in. These yearly or biyearly goals should serve as the guiding force for each day's lesson. Without them, it will be difficult for you to know what students need to accomplish each day. Furthermore, it will be much easier for students to produce work of accuracy and value if they know, with as much precision as possible, what you are expecting of them. Therefore, it is important for you to decide on the goals and their sequence. Once this is done, it's important to write the goals in language that is clear, age appropriate, and communicative to students.

⊕ THE STRATEGY

Learning goals for units (and the unit goal area used to develop learning goals for each lesson) should be written in the form of what is essential for students to *know* (K), *understand* (U), and be able to *do* (D) by the end of each lesson. The *know* of this learning goal refers to facts and details that students will need to attain by the end of the lesson or unit (Tomlinson, 2001; Tomlinson & Imbeau, 2014). Dates, names, and vocabulary terms are all examples of things to know. For example, students might need to know key dates or figures related to World War I, vocabulary terms related to the digestive system, key terms related to lunar and solar eclipses, or the elements of a fairy tale.

The knowledge facet of KUD also includes the steps in a procedure (Tomlinson, 2001; Tomlinson & Imbeau, 2014). For example, by the end of a lesson, students might be expected to know how to calculate percentage or volume or area, how to write an expository text, or how to analyze primary documents in history. Students need to know the steps involved in a procedure prior to actualizing the procedure or skill. "To know" can often be replaced with "to memorize." Some might believe that knowing or memorizing information has little value in the 21st century given our easy access to technology, and in particular Google and other search engines. However, to become an expert in any field, and to have the ability to think deeply about concepts, the ability to manipulate knowledge is essential. Imagine communicating a list of symptoms to your doctor who needs to look up the definition of each symptom in order to problem solve and suggest an intervention. Similarly, imagine your financial planner, insurance salesperson, or lawyer being unable to engage in a conversation about different scenarios that you present without depending on Google. In order to have a deep-level conversation and to manipulate information, one simply needs to master basic facts. It is only at this point that complex problem solving using these facts can occur (Hattie, 2008).

Finally, knowledge is binary, meaning that the student response is either correct or incorrect. Of course, this superficial knowledge is not the end goal; rather, it's only the beginning. In order to engage in deep learning, a student must learn foundational knowledge first (Tomlinson, 2001; Tomlinson & Imbeau, 2014). Returning for a moment to the questions outlined in the introduction that lead to purposeful teaching, the explicit articulating of steps students need to follow to carry out a procedure is essential for students to ultimately become independent learners. If you are able to list the steps required to find area or volume or to complete a problem, you can then model for students how to complete the procedure by following these steps. If you teach the steps explicitly, stating one step at a time and then, while illuminating each step, completing an example on the board, the students should manage to follow these same steps when completing a problem on their own. This begins with the clear articulating of the goals—what students need to *know* in order to master the learning goals.

Next, teachers should also be able to explain to students *why* they are learning what they're learning. The *understanding* of the learning goal in KUD is meant to communicate to students the overarching concept and why students are learning what they're learning (Tomlinson, 2001; Tomlinson & Imbeau, 2014; Tomlinson & Moon, 2013). It's important to write the understanding in terms of "students will understand that . . ." because this contextualizes the learning and provides students with the authentic context (Tomlinson, 2001; Tomlinson & Imbeau, 2014; Tomlinson & Moon, 2013). For example, in a unit on seasons and eclipses, students might need to learn facts about lunar and solar eclipses. As part of this learning, they will likely need to know the spatial relationships of the sun, Earth, and moon during each of these two events. However, the question students might ask is, "Why is the order important?" Learning that is not contextualized is often forgotten, and we often take for granted either that students know this information or that it's unimportant for them (Tomlinson, 2001; Tomlinson & Imbeau, 2014; Tomlinson & Moon, 2013). Therefore, students would benefit from understanding that in a solar eclipse, the moon passes between the sun and the Earth, blocking the sun's light. This element of the learning goal helps students understand the purpose of their learning.

When we instruct students to learn facts, details, and procedures, but don't explain why this knowledge is essential, why they need to learn it, and who uses this knowledge in real life, the learning has limited value for the students. As another example, in a unit on fairy tales, students might need to know the elements of a fairy tale, but contextualizing this for students is critical. You could explain to your students why it is important to study fairy tales and what we learn from them. For example, you might mention that we learn much about ourselves when we read fairy tales, as they speak of relevant human conditions such as love, friendship, or fear. Also, fairy tales often help us to better understand challenges in our own life.

The third and final element of the learning goal is *doing*, which indicates what the students will be able to do as a result of having learned the knowledge and having grappled with the deeper concepts and understandings (Tomlinson, 2001; Tomlinson & Imbeau, 2014; Tomlinson & Moon, 2013). Therefore, using the example of the seasons and eclipses, at the close of this lesson, students would be expected to draw a diagram of a lunar eclipse and explain its components. With regard to the fairy tale unit, at the end of a day's lesson, the teacher could ask students to write out the elements of a fairy tale and explain the author's purpose for writing fairy tales. They could also be asked to think of a fairy tale they know and compare it to some aspect of their life.

Students should show their mastery at each stage in the learning process. At the start of a unit, students may only be expected to list the elements of a narrative. Therefore, mastery does not refer to summative achievement of the goals, but rather is a check along the way to ensure that the subgoals or content knowledge have been learned. This very important practice of formative assessment will be addressed in chapter 5 (page 89).

This concept of gradual accomplishment and evaluation of goals along the way can be compared to a road trip. It is essential to know the destination—or to "begin with the end in mind"—because if you don't, it will be impossible to proclaim that you have arrived. Furthermore, having a destination is essential, but equally important is the establishment of checkpoints along the way to ensure that you are headed in the right direction. This is what Frey, Hattie, and Fisher (2018) refer to as success criteria. It is great to turn off the road and observe the scenery, but without learning goals and success criteria, it is difficult, if at all possible, to discriminate between veering off the road and driving toward your destination.

Learning goals need to state exactly what you want students to know, understand, and be able to do by the end of each unit and lesson. For example, you may want your students to know the definition of literary devices and understand that literary devices enrich a text, and by the end of the lesson you may want your students to actually use literary devices in their written text. However, what I have seen many times is a lack of clarity with regard to the goal. Teachers may implicitly know that they want their students to use literary devices, but their instruction instead focuses on identifying literary devices but not how to actually apply them in a written text. Knowing how to identify literary devices requires a different instructional set than being able to use them in writing. Therefore, having a clear sense of the goal and how students will show mastery is critical to students' success.

Learning goals should also be challenging relative to the students' mastery of the topic, and they should be shared and explained to the students. Finally, using these learning goals as your blueprint for each unit and lesson would be helpful. Throughout the unit, you may find it beneficial to return to these learning goals by showing students where you are along the way and bringing them back to these learning goals as they learn to master each goal. After all, what a great feeling of accomplishment for you and your student when you both realize what you have accomplished!

A MODEL OF EFFECTIVE USE OF LEARNING GOALS THROUGHOUT A LESSON

In a history class, the teacher began by writing the learning goals on the board. She had identified specific goals for *knowledge, understanding*, and *doing* related to statewide interventions in cases of, for example, natural disasters and human disasters. (While this occurred prior to COVID-19, this topic would be very relevant in a post-pandemic world.) Under *knowledge*, the teacher listed the times in which states must intervene; for example, a hundred-acre forest fire might be such an occasion, whereas a small fire in a house would be a job for municipal firefighters, not the state. The *understandings* were listed as follows: students will understand that states must make wise decisions about when they do and do not intervene, as these decisions affect availability and allocation of resources within the state. Finally, for the *doing* portion, students were ask to summarize each of four cases and present authentic examples from current situations for each one.

continued →

As the teacher presented the knowledge (facts), and as students worked throughout the lesson, the key learning goals were addressed. The teacher referred back to each of the goals to indicate to the students what they had learned. The learning was visible (according to Hattie [2008, 2012]) because quick, formative evaluations were conducted throughout the lesson. For example, the teacher conducted quick evaluations using technology such as check-ins via Kahoot (www.kahoot.com) and Plickers (https://get.plickers.com). It was evident from the quick formative assessments that the students had mastered the goals. Equally exciting was how engaged the students were throughout the lesson. Finally, it was wonderful to see how accomplished the teacher felt, having begun the lesson in the most purposeful way with clear goals that were explicitly stated during the learning sequence. Finally, having students succeed, as evidenced by the formative assessment, was pure joy to the teacher.

When teachers begin to think in terms of student learning rather than teacher objectives, something magical unfolds: the teacher embarks on a total metamorphosis or transformation in teaching. Why do some teachers struggle so significantly to develop learning goals? For one thing, when you plan your lessons, you might be thinking in terms of what you'll teach rather than what students will learn (Darling-Hammond, 2007; Marzano, 2009a; Peterson, Marx, & Clark, 1978; Wiggins & McTighe, 2007). As the teacher, you have almost complete control over what it is that you will teach, be it chapter 3, or fractions, or the causes of World War II, or stars and constellations. What you have far less control over, however, is what students will learn (Hattie, 2012).

When you clearly articulate student learning goals, you have the ability to know who has and who has not mastered these goals as indicated by ongoing formative assessments. With this information, you may feel the weight of needing to respond to those students who have not mastered the goals and to those students who have exceeded the goals (even before the lesson begins). There's a new sense of accountability when we transition from what we'll do as teachers to what students will be able to master. However, with time, it will become easier to address the needs of the students who have not learned the target goals. One possible solution is to plan a ten-minute independent activity for the students who seem to have mastered the learning goals (as evidenced by the formative assessment; see chapter 5, page 89, for additional details). During these ten minutes, you can loop back to work with students who need some guidance. Clearly, ten minutes is a short amount of time, but if this is done on a regular basis, the gap will be minimal in most cases. Of course, there will always be students who require additional out-of-class support. Another suggestion is to engage in anchor activities, which will be discussed in greater detail in chapter 6 (page 109).

Another area of challenge in the development of learning goals is how to articulate them in a way that reflects what students actually need to walk away with (Donovan & Bransford, 2005; Wiggins & McTighe, 1998). Goals are often tacit in the minds of teachers. Teachers can often be heard saying, "I know, more or less, what they need to be able to do." But this level of implied and not overtly articulated goals becomes a challenge. Simply put, we can't evaluate what isn't clear to us.

KEEP IT SIMPLE

From my experience working with teachers on the development of learning goals, the challenge comes not from an inability to articulate the learning goals but from the difficulty of trying to think about learning goals in too sophisticated a way. I've seen teachers initially struggle, trying to fit what they more or less want students to accomplish into clearly and explicitly articulated goals. But when we talk it out and then try putting these goals on paper, it becomes much easier. The trick is to think as simply as possible about what you want students to accomplish, and to think about the goals from the vantage point of the students. For example, in a lesson on constellations, what knowledge or facts do students need to have?

The next question I ask teachers is what they say to a student who asks, "Why do I need to know this?" This forms the understanding of the *why*, and when we provide the students with the why, they tend to be more interested in learning.

Finally, I tell teachers, what could you ask students to do at the end of the lesson to indicate that they have learned what you intended them to learn? These end-of-lesson formative evaluations are small markers to ascertain whether or not students are acquiring the knowledge, skills, and understanding along the way (Sadler, 1989; Stiggins & DuFour, 2009).

continued →

There are many options as to where you can display these goals: for example, the first slide of a slideshow, the board, or a movable whiteboard. For young students, who may not have learned to read, you can state the learning goals in just a few simple and age-appropriate words at the start of the lesson.

Given the essential role that learning goals play in successful learning (Gonzalez & Leticia, 2013; Jansen, Bartell, & Berk, 2009), it's vital that they become a part of every lesson. For example, you can begin a lesson by explaining to students that by the end of class *they will be able to* calculate the perimeter of a rectangle—a shape that could represent your backyard. *This is important because* you would need to build a fence around your yard if, for example, you wanted to enclose your pool. In order to do this, you would explain to your students, *they will need to know* the steps involved in calculating the perimeter. This is a clearly articulated goal that sets up an explicit structure around a lesson. With this clearly articulated goal, you and your students will know where it is you need to go during the course of the lesson so that by the end, students will be able to calculate perimeter. It also sets you up so that by the end of class you will know who has met this goal and who has not. In contrast, a poorly articulated goal would sound something like "By the end of the lesson, students will understand how to calculate perimeter." This is a poorly articulated goal as there is no clear statement as to what students will be able to do to show mastery of the goal.

At first, it might be daunting for teachers to need to hold themselves accountable for the specific mastery of learning goals. However, using learning goals as a teaching strategy is one of the most effective ways of identifying which students have and have not mastered the goals at the culmination of each lesson (Cleary et al., 2017; Wiggins & McTighe, 1998). Why wait for the summative evaluation—when it's likely too late to help—to learn that some students failed to master the goals? It's much easier to remediate smaller gaps than to wait until these gaps become chasms (Beecher & Sweeny, 2008; Rose & Meyer, 2002).

To aid you in the creation and communication of learning goals, figure 2.1 lists several key things to remember. The list might seem obvious at first glance, but given how these are often overlooked, the consolidation of these items seemed necessary (Dean et al., 2012; Marzano & Brown, 2009; Wiggins & McTighe, 2007). Keep this list handy as you set your learning goals for each unit and lesson. For examples of clear and well-phrased learning goals, see figure 2.2.

1. Clearly post learning objectives
Your learning goals should never be a secret, so don't leave students guessing. Without learning goals, your students might eventually give up. You should write these goals down and place them in a prominent place in your classroom. That way, students can reflect on the goals throughout the lesson and evaluate how they are doing in relation to the goals. As well, you can focus on the goals that you need to address throughout the lesson.
2. Make your learning objectives relevant
Iterate your learning objectives before each lesson. By your bringing attention to the learning goals, the students will see, very visibly, what they need to pay attention to.
3. Write the learning goals in simple language
Keep them short, sweet, and simple. Think about transmitting these goals to a student. If you are concerned that they might be too complex, they probably are. In the younger classrooms, the goals should have few words, and images if needed.
4. Make sure they are really objectives or goals, not activities
Don't confuse objectives, or what the students need to master (for example, *describe the author's perspective in the introduction*), with activities, or what students will be doing in class in pursuit of the goals (for example, *read the introduction of this book*).
5. Ensure your learning goals drive the lesson
Often, teachers have great activities, but they have nothing to do with the learning objective, so be sure that you align your activities and assessments with objectives.

Figure 2.1: Key things to remember when creating and communicating learning goals.

*Visit **go.SolutionTree.com/instruction** for a free reproducible version of this figure.*

Know	Understand	Do
How to tell time (to the hour)	*That* time helps us to organize our day, and also helps us make sure that we arrive to places such as playdates with a friend on time	*Identify* the time indicated on the clock (to the hour).
How to multiply by 2, 5, and 9	*That* multiplication is a shortcut for addition	*Multiply* by 2, 5, and 9.
How to use a grid on a map to find latitude and longitude	*That* grids are useful indicators to find latitude and longitude on a map	*Find* latitude and longitude of the following countries on the map using the grid.

Figure 2.2: Sample learning goals (KUD).

continued →

Know	Understand	Do
Definition of literary devices (simile, metaphor, personification) How to identify a literary device	*That* authors use literary devices to persuade, entertain, describe, and connect to the reader	*Define* the following literary devices (simile, hyperbole, personification). *Identify* the literary device in the passage and identify what you think the author's purpose was in using the particular device.
When perimeter is used How to calculate perimeter	*That* calculating perimeter of a room enables us to put wall-to-wall carpet on the floor with precision, and also enables us to know if a pool will fit in our backyard	*Calculate* the perimeter of the room.
The elements of a persuasive essay The vocabulary used to help us persuade	*That* effective authors use logical organization to convey their message *That* clear and convincing language will help you convince your reader of your point of view	*List* the elements of a persuasive essay. *Put* the following words in a sentence.
The names and characteristics of the planets in terms of size, surface, and specific properties	*That* the solar system is made up of diverse planets, each one with its own unique characteristics	*List* all of the planets and three characteristics of each one that highlights its size, surface, and properties.

THE IMPORTANCE OF ALIGNING THE INSTRUCTIONAL ACTIVITY WITH THE LEARNING GOALS

A teacher once invited me into his classroom to observe a tenth-grade history lesson. He had planned an activity and wanted my feedback.

Walking down the hallway, I heard the excitement of students who were clearly engaged in a fun activity. In the class, students were using Popsicle sticks to build explorer Jacques Cartier's boat—a fun activity, no doubt, but unlikely to address the learning goal that the teacher had previously determined, which was to identify the specific challenges that Cartier and his team underwent on their voyages to North America.

There are specific strategies that you can use, such as providing clear learning goals and tracking student progress (Chappuis & Stiggins, 2002; Marzano, 2009a), then celebrating student success. When these strategies are embraced, it creates a classroom culture where students are motivated to take more responsibility for their own learning (Brush & Saye, 2000; Marzano & Brown, 2009).

THE EXCITEMENT FOR ALL STUDENTS WHEN GOALS ARE CLEARLY ARTICULATED AND REACHED

In a third-grade English language arts class, each student in the class was given a fluency goal with the number of words he or she needed to be able to read per minute without error. Fluency is the bridge between decoding and comprehension, and thus reading fluency is essential for students to be able to understand what they are reading (Pikulski & Chard, 2005). When reading is disfluent, too much energy is expended on trying to read the words, thus leaving little energy for understanding what the text is about. In this class, every time the students had reached their fluency goal, they were invited to stand at the front of the class to announce their success. Once stated, the class erupted in applause. The look on each student's face said it all: *I was presented with a learning goal—and I made it!*

If there is one consistent takeaway from all my years of observing teachers in classrooms from elementary school to high school, it is this: lesson goals are at the heart of teaching and learning. Teaching with purpose means thinking deeply and constantly about what you want students to achieve and thinking about how you will get there. It also means communicating these goals to students because you are mindful about how important this is to students' success. When you begin with the end in mind, you are able to ensure that learning is focused and that there is a purpose resulting in breakthrough moments for even the hardest-to-reach students.

To begin implementing these ideas, you can choose from some of the strategies listed in the reproducible "Strategies for Establishing and Communicating Learning Goals" on page 41, or print your own blank version of this chart at **go .SolutionTree.com/instruction** and jot down some of your own ideas.

⌐ NEXT STEPS

Look at an upcoming unit you're going to teach soon, and determine what you want students to know, understand, and be able to do. Record these in the reproducible "Template for Establishing and Communicating Learning Goals" found on page 42. Depending on the unit and your grade level and content area, you might also want to break down the goals lesson by lesson. Be sure to follow the list of key things to remember when creating and communicating learning goals in figure 2.1 (page 37) as you're planning and teaching.

Strategies for Establishing and Communicating Learning Goals

STRATEGY	EXAMPLE
Clearly post learning goals.	Post the learning goals on the whiteboard. This way students can use them as a reference throughout the lesson. If you are using a portal such as Google Classroom, post the learning goals there for each lesson.
Make the learning goals relevant.	Identify for the students why they are learning this information. Ask: "How will knowing this impact their life?" For example, you could write, "Students will understand that learning about fractions will help them make sure that they will get their fair share of the chocolate brownies or pizza."
Use simple language.	These goals are written for students, so keep the language simple. For example, "By the end of the lesson, you will know the steps that you need to follow in order to add fractions with like denominators. You will understand that fractions are important because the world is divided into parts (for example, you can break an orange into slices). You will be able to add fractions with like denominators."
Make sure that your learning goals are actual goals and not activities.	For example, the goal should be, "Students will be able to write a paragraph to convince the teacher to extend their lunch period," rather than "Students will read two examples of persuasive paragraphs."
Make sure that your goals drive the lesson.	If you want students to be able to describe the challenges experienced by Jacques Cartier (a Canadian explorer who came from France), students should be examining what factors led to the different challenges and not doing an activity such as designing the boat that he took during his voyages. Alternatively, if you want students to be able to write a descriptive text in a second language, the lesson focus should be on key descriptive vocabulary and sentence structure, and not completing pages in a workbook.

Template for Establishing and Communicating Learning Goals

Unit Title:

Date of Implementation:

Grade Level:

List all goals for the unit in the table below. A unit is approximately ten lessons.

Identify the date that you plan to teach each of these learning goals

KNOW	UNDERSTAND	DO	DATE BY WHICH THE GOALS WILL BE TAUGHT

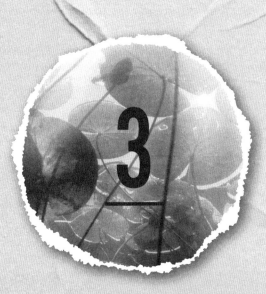

Incorporating Strategic
Teaching and Learning

Once a teacher has established his or her classroom as an ecosystem, providing students with a learning environment conducive to success, what does that teacher need to *do* so that students become successful learners, master learning goals, and feel as though they are capable students whose efforts will reap results? Using my in-the-trenches experience spanning three decades in elementary and high school classrooms, and relying heavily on evidence-based research by leading education researchers, I have learned that there are tried-and-true strategies that, when applied with consistency, help students remain engaged and learning. The most effective teachers have two things in common: (1) they are committed to teaching strategies that are known to work in an intentional, mindful, and purposeful way, and (2) they engage with their students in an empathetic and positive manner.

This chapter begins by discussing some problems you may have seen in your classroom as a result of a lack of strategic teaching. It will then delve into the principle of *incorporating strategic teaching and learning* and discuss the research and evidence surrounding this practice. It then describes several strategies you can use for each stage of the *three stages of learning* model as you begin applying this principle in your classroom. The chapter concludes with a plan for next steps you can take over the coming months.

⚡ THE CHALLENGE

These days, the idea of "Talk less so they'll listen more" rushes back at me every time I'm in a classroom where a teacher speaks for too long about a concept or procedure. It's not hard to know when the talking is going on too long, because the students inevitably will get that "lost in space" look or start fidgeting around in their seats—or even worse, become disruptive. Regardless of how passionate we are about our subject and how clearly we instruct our students, when we talk too much, we lose them (Hattie, 2003; Porath, 2014).

When we talk for too long in our attempt to explain a new concept (often referred to as *frontal teaching*), you may hear your students start to mumble, "How did you get that number? Isn't that a line—why are you calling it a segment? How do we know which formula to choose from that whole list? Can't we just use metaphor and simile interchangeably?" Comments such as these are signals that the content you're teaching has not yet been learned by all. Pay attention to the signals and let your radar kick in. Perhaps the student has become distracted or disengaged and has stopped paying attention. This happens—and it happens in all classrooms, those of novice as well as experienced teachers. But how we respond to these signals is what's key.

Equally troubling is when we've spent time explaining how to proceed with a new skill, only to find, when the students begin working on their own, that they are unable to follow the procedure independently. Hands go up flailing in the air, and students begin asking for assistance—questions such as, "Where do I put that number?" or "Remind me what I need to write in my topic sentence!" abound in the classroom. Oftentimes I see the frustrated look on the teacher's face, as if to say, "Didn't I just show you how to do this? Why are there so many students struggling?" There are some simple yet very effective steps to follow in the process of teaching new content or a new skill that, when followed, can significantly reduce these frustrating and challenging problems that are common in many classrooms.

✤ THE PRINCIPLE

Teaching is most effective when it is *strategic* and when lesson goals are presented with intent and delivered with effective methodology so that the learners can master the goals (Seidel et al., 2005). The concept of strategic teaching will be mentioned throughout this chapter and is an essential component of effective teaching. Simply put, strategic teaching refers to an explicit (not tacit) teaching process whereby students are clearly informed that they are going to learn the steps required to master a skill, and the steps are clearly and explicitly presented to students using an "I do, we do, you do one, you do many" approach (which will be explained in this chapter). Additionally, we want students to take what they learn with them when they move on from us.

An excellent way to imbue independent thinking is for the teacher to talk less and allow students the space to expand their thinking, ask questions, and make sense of the puzzle of information (Hattie, 2003). Many years ago, in an undergraduate course on inclusive education, a student summed up this idea by saying, "So basically, teachers need to stop talking before the students stop listening."

So, what can you do when you are no doubt under time pressure to complete lesson content, units, chapters, and all the rest? Although talking less to get more done may seem paradoxical, it's been showcased time and again that when you slow down your lessons, you get more done *well* (Hattie, 2003; Porath, 2014; Rowe, 1986; Wood, 2002). In contrast, when your students can no longer process an abundance of new information, continuing to press forward is just time lost. Teaching methodologically requires teachers to be mindful of what material they need to teach and then adopt a strategy aligned with the type of learning students require (Bloom, Englehart, Furst, Hill, & Krathwohl, 1956; Hattie, 2003; Tomlinson, 2014). It is important to begin each unit by identifying the learning content that is essential to teach and for students to learn. In their book *Integrating Differentiated Instruction and Understanding by Design*, Tomlinson and McTighe (2006) identify that, as teachers, we can't teach everything. Therefore, we constantly need to make decisions about what is most important to teach in the sense of what will be most "durable and useful" for students in the future (Tomlinson & McTighe, 2006, p. 40). Equally essential to the overall effectiveness of the learning process is for you to be mindful with regards to *what* is being taught (whether you're teaching new knowledge, which is declarative, or skills, which are procedural) and to be purposeful in terms of *how* to effectively teach it.

While it's effective for students to be challenged, there is a line, often quite clear, that separates effective problem solving and inquiry from confusion and bewilderment. Allowing more time for students to be active players in their own learning, ask questions, and actively and methodically process fundamental new information effectively helps diminish negative outcomes (Hattie, 2003; Porath, 2014; Wood, 2002). Ultimately, teaching that is purposeful and intentional will go a long way toward the development of student mastery and confidence in learning (Hattie, 2003; Loughran, 2013).

To be a purposeful and strategic teacher who will produce strategic students, specific stages or processes of learning are essential. It's especially important to understand the kinds of learning experiences that lead to *transfer*, defined as the ability to extend what has been learned in one context to new contexts (Byrnes, 1996; Fisher, Frey, & Hattie, 2016; Hattie, Biggs, & Purdie, 1996). I have seen the most experienced teachers miss this vital step in the learning process. They may teach information or facts clearly and with purpose, but then miss teaching *transfer* to new contexts. This transfer is essential because, after all, students' ability to apply information within new situations is the essence of true mastery.

⊕ THE STRATEGY

When teachers back away from being the only or main voice in the classroom for an extended period of time, students become active participants and learn to take responsibility for their learning (Hattie, 2003, 2012; Porath, 2014; Wood, 2002). At the beginning of a lesson or when new material is being introduced, the teacher has a prominent role in the delivery of the content. But as the student acquires the new information and must demonstrate proficiency with skill acquisition, the responsibility for learning gradually shifts from teacher-directed instruction to student-processing activities, with decreasing levels of teacher guidance and input. You can continue to model, question, prompt, and cue students, but as students continue in the process, they should rely more on themselves and their classmates and less on the teacher to complete the learning task (Levy, 2007). Truly mastering teaching means knowing how much guidance to give, when to give that guidance, and how to then gradually decrease your role and allow the student to become more autonomous.

One strategy many teachers utilize to help students connect with their learning and achieve transfer is *problem-based learning* (Savery, 2015). Problem-based learning involves a *bottom-up approach*, which highlights the reason *why* students are going to be learning what they are about to learn. It provides them with an authentic task that needs to be resolved at the end of the unit, which serves to motivate the student with the understanding that there is a purpose for the learning and that it is not solely to complete a test or exam at the end. As I will explain in this chapter, these authentic tasks are both engaging and meaningful to students because they are working toward a meaningful end, usually by creating something that also has value outside the four walls of the classroom (Darling-Hammond & Snyder, 2000; Grisham-Brown, Hallam, & Brookshire, 2006; Wiggins, 1990, 1998). But in order to be able to move to this stage, teachers must also provide students with *top-down learning*, which is an intentional, step-by-step approach to teaching knowledge and skills essential for higher-level mastery (Archer & Hughes, 2010; Biggs, 1999; Zarrabi, 2017). This approach is absent in some of the applications of problem-based learning. The top-down process refers to when teachers provide explicit instruction, offering students unambiguous explanations and directly teaching students the foundational knowledge that will enable them to develop proficiency in skill acquisition and effective transfer (Biggs, 1996, 1999). In the age of technology, you might feel as though students no longer need to master facts because a quick Google search will provide the answer. However, as Hattie (2008) notes in his study of effective teaching practices, in order to become an expert in any field, the ability to gain quick mastery of facts, with the ability to manipulate those facts, is an essential element required for higher-order and complex problem solving. We should perhaps try to discourage students from being so quick to access Google and instead challenge them to reach into the annals of their minds and do their own internal Google search.

In order to become an expert in any field, there is knowledge and basic skill that must be acquired (Collins, Brown, & Holum, 1991; Dennen & Burner, 2008; Palincsar, 1986; VanLehn, 1988). A recent visit to an English classroom illustrated this point beautifully. It was the first day of their new unit, and the group of eight-year-olds in the English class were dressed up like animal activists. They knew that they were going to save animals that were at risk of becoming extinct, and they were excitedly awaiting this monumental task. It would ultimately involve a visit from a professional activist and a lot of letter writing and other tasks that activists typically engage in. But to begin, there was to be considerable frontloading of essential information and skills, which would enable the students to confidently take on this authentic and very important task. In this scenario, the teacher gave students initial context to what they would be doing and why they would be doing it. The students understood how to do what the teacher was asking of them and why. With this understanding, they attached meaning to the tasks. With these capabilities, students could then begin to transfer what they learned to diverse situations and take on varying perspectives. The hope was that the students eventually would be able to engage in situations that require them to think and act like experts.

This top-down approach, which takes students from being novice learners to experts, is methodical, direct, and explicitly teacher modeled. It begins with you maintaining initial control over the learning situation and gradually transitioning to an environment whereby the control and responsibility for learning belongs to the students. This transition from teacher responsibility to student responsibility is essential to effective student mastery (Biggs, 1996, 1999). With this gradual release of responsibility, the students begin with a sense of confidence in their learning, even though they are not yet fully capable to engage in the task, and they end with a larger sense of confidence because they are now able to independently master the task (Biggs, 1996, 1999). This chapter will highlight the transition from teacher responsibility to student responsibility.

There are three stages in the learning process that take a student from being a novice, new to the learning goals, to an expert able to apply the goals in multiple authentic contexts (Hattie, 2012). These three stages are (1) surface or new knowledge, (2) consolidation and automaticity and the beginning stages of deep learning, and (3) transfer, all of which are important and necessary components for teaching and learning to be effective. Fisher et al. (2016) highlight the importance of designing classroom learning around these stages, which enable students to effectively transition from surface learning to consolidation of knowledge and, ultimately, to transfer. These three stages of learning are described in the following sections.

Stage 1: Surface or New Knowledge

How can you impart new knowledge so you begin the process of lighting a fire, not just filling a pail? How should material be presented so that different students being taught are able to learn it, retain it, and use it in the real world? This has been and continues to be a source of challenge for both the novice and the expert teacher. There are three elements to consider during stage 1: (1) utilizing preassessments, (2) explicitly teaching new knowledge, and (3) slowing down instruction to teach effectively.

Utilizing Preassessments

Preassessment is essential because it indicates to you whether the students have previously mastered the skills, knowledge, or understandings that must precede what you are about to teach. Equally important, preassessment helps you monitor student progress and measure student growth (Hattie, 2012; Hockett & Doubet, 2013). The preassessment also serves to identify misconceptions that students might have (Hattie, 2012; Hockett & Doubet, 2013; McTighe & O'Connor, 2009). In fact, misconceptions are often more concerning than unmastered skills or knowledge, because when students begin a new unit of study with misconceptions, they'll likely map new knowledge onto these misconceptions. It is important to identify and correct misconceptions before additional faulty learning can occur. Examples of preassessments at an elementary level could be providing students with a fraction example to complete (such as $\frac{1}{2} + \frac{2}{4} = ?$), asking students to write a sentence telling you what they ate for breakfast to assess their knowledge of sentence structure and syntax, or asking students to define the term *decomposer*, *habitat*, or *mitosis*.

A typical concern of many teachers, and a main reason why they avoid preassessments, is that they believe they have insufficient time to conduct a preassessment

(Marzano, Marzano, & Pickering, 2003). However, you will save no time by beginning a unit or chapter with the faulty assumption that students have mastered or have gaps in prerequisite skills. Unfortunately, there is no other option because you will need to take the time later on, once these lags in knowledge and skill interfere with student learning. Additionally, preassessments need not take up very much time. Preassessments are not graded; instead, they're simple, short, and sweet, and they typically take only about ten minutes to complete (Hattie, 2012; Hockett & Doubet, 2013).

Following a preassessment is often a good time to utilize *anchor activities.* Anchor activities will be discussed in greater detail in chapter 6 (page 109), but an example of an anchor activity for a lesson on fractions might be to provide students who have shown mastery of a concept a more challenging task (such as creating multiple fraction word problems) while you spend time reviewing the basic steps involved in solving a simple fraction problem for the rest of the class. As part of preassessment, when you identify who has not mastered the fundamental prerequisite knowledge or skills, you could take a little time to work with these students early in the new unit, or even before it starts, to provide them with a minilesson that focuses on these critical skills while other students work on an anchor activity. For some weaker students, they may require only a review of the previously learned material. However, other cases may need basic reteaching of the content in a different, clearer, more tangible way. If the required content centers on the steps in a problem or skill, the student may require very explicit teaching of the steps.

Ultimately, asking students to demonstrate their understanding of the subject matter is critical to the learning process (Hattie, 2008, 2012). When you routinely engage in preassessments of prerequisite skills, you can identify those who struggle early on, which will result in the students receiving the support they need early, avoiding a situation where the gap grows into a chasm too difficult to remediate.

Explicitly Teaching New Knowledge

Once you have completed the preassessment and identified and addressed any lags in knowledge, you can begin the explicit teaching of new knowledge. Many researchers posit the benefits of beginning a new unit with a clear and explicit presentation of new information (Archer & Hughes, 2010; Brophy & Good, 1986; Marzano, 2007; Swanson, 2001). For example, Robert Marzano (2007) tested instructional strategies for teaching vocabulary to see if they result in quantitative achievement gains, and he found that the most important teacher-controlled factor related to student success is to tell students explicitly what they need to know and then show them what they eventually need to be able to do on their own. Another essential aspect of this phase—presentation of new knowledge—is that the knowledge needs to be presented by a reliable source. When you begin a lesson or unit that is based on factual information by asking students what they think they know about the topic, a lot of misinformation will inevitably circulate around the classroom and eventually become fused with the accurate information (Hattie, 2012; Hockett & Doubet, 2013; McTighe & O'Connor, 2009). It is much better to ensure that only accurate, factual information is presented at this early stage. The chance for students to demonstrate knowledge will come later.

SHARING MISINFORMATION IN THE CLASSROOM

Two examples of early sharing of misinformation come to mind: one in a first-grade class and one in an eighth-grade class. In the first-grade class, the teacher was beginning a unit on whales. She began by asking students to share with their classmates what they knew about whales. In true first-grade fashion, many students raised their hands, only too happy to share with the class that "whales are big fish that live in the ocean and are very scary and dangerous." Of course, no first-grade teacher, or any teacher for that matter, would want to correct these engaged and motivated students in front of their classmates, so much misinformation was passed around in the lively discussion about whales. In the second example, the eighth-grade teacher began a mathematics unit by asking students what a ray, a line, and a segment were. Here again, a lot of misinformation was shared with students.

Both of these teachers were very experienced, having taught these grades for over ten years. But both made the mistake of allowing misinformation to be shared in the explicit teaching stage, allowing this misinformation to be shared with all students in the classroom. This mistake can be avoided by both novice and experienced teachers by being *purposeful* in one's teaching. The questions to ask are, "What do I want students to learn?" and "What is the best way for me to teach it?" Following this, of course, is, "How will I know if they've learned?" In order to effectively teach new knowledge, it must come solely from a reliable source (Marzano, 2007).

When a topic is factual and conceptual (such as "What is the definition of capitalism?" or "How long does it take for the Earth to orbit around the sun?") or procedural (such as "What are the steps that need to be followed when solving an equation?" or "What are the elements in a narrative story?"), the information must come directly from a reliable source such as the teacher, a practitioner in the field, a textbook, or a reliable internet site such as Khan Academy (www .khanacademy.org). This isn't true, however, for a subjective examination of a topic such as the meaning of friendship or success, or an experience with bullying or stereotyping. With these, there's no definitive right or wrong answer, so there's no problem with students sharing their opinions at this early stage.

Students need to receive new knowledge in such a way that they're able to consolidate the information in memory (Sousa, 2016). According to David Sousa (2016), *memory consolidation* is the process of encoding information or processing newly presented information, and it is imperative to enable learners to hold on to new knowledge. Memory consolidation doesn't occur instantly, and certainly not as a result of having heard the information presented only once. At this point, teachers would need to pause their instruction and provide students with an opportunity to recode the information or summarize it in their own words.

Essential to memory consolidation when teaching students a strategy to master a skill is the naming of the strategy. For example, a very effective strategy to comprehend text is to ask yourself a question while you read to evaluate if you understand the text. If you are able to ask and then answer the question, there's a good chance that you're comprehending what you are reading. For example, imagine students are reading a text about a young girl who woke up early one morning excited to begin her first day of horseback riding school. She ate her cereal as quickly as she possibly could, put on her riding gear, and ran out the front door. Students would be encouraged to ask themselves a question to assess their understanding of the paragraph. A good question to ask might be "What was the young girl excited about?" When teaching this strategy, teachers can explain that students should think of asking themselves questions while reading, much like the questions that teachers might ask on a comprehension quiz. If teachers want students to use this strategy consistently and effectively, students need to be told that they are learning a strategy and that it is called *questioning*. Students should be shown how to use the strategy and then given practice to apply it.

Finally, students should be praised when they apply strategies effectively. Teaching a strategy can be likened to giving a gift—something one gives to a recipient so it can then be used independently. If you give a gift but it can only be used when the giver is present, that isn't much of a gift. Likewise, the strategy must be taught slowly, methodically, and intentionally so that ultimately the students will be able to apply it independent of the teacher and in many contexts. Master teachers teach methodically, with a clear articulation of steps and with lots of practice (Archer & Hughes, 2010; Peterson & Corneaux, 1987). The students then hear the teacher's voice guiding them through the process. Leaving your voice behind with your students to guide them through the simple and the difficult tasks they will encounter when you are not there is the best gift teachers can provide to their students.

Slowing Down Instruction

The third element to consider when you engage in this stage of teaching is the need to slow down and allow students the opportunity to create their own symbolic representation of the new information. A common phenomenon seen in classrooms is teachers explaining a concept for too long without stopping to allow students the opportunity to empty their pails (Sousa, 2016). Shorter learning sessions are more effective to the storage of memory than longer sessions (Tse et al., 2007).

In order for you to present information to students in a clear and coherent fashion, you first need to read about it. Do some research if necessary, or perhaps speak to other teachers to find out how they teach new concepts and procedures. For you to teach a new concept, you need to process and symbolically represent the information yourself, and it is important that you afford students this same opportunity. When a teacher presents too much information frontally, with no opportunity for students to make sense of it for themselves, ask questions, or ponder ideas presented, it overwhelms their memory systems and becomes difficult to integrate and store for later use (Huitt, 2003; Hultberg, Calonge, & Lee, 2018; Lewis, 2016). In order for information to be learned, brains need to reorganize and modify that information. Further, Fancourt and Holmes (2020) and Squire (1992) identify rehearsal and repetition as critical to the formation of memory. These elements are necessary for the consolidation of new knowledge. Chunking and recoding are two strategies teachers can use at this stage to help students consolidate information and retain it to memory for future use.

CHUNKING

Chunking refers to presenting new content in small, easily processable sections (Marzano, 2007). It makes more efficient use of short-term memory by grouping information and thus helping students avoid information overload. It presents new information in small, digestible bites, so students can take in the information more easily. Chunking is an excellent strategy for helping students solidify information and retain rapid access to it (Huitt, 2003; Mayzner & Gabriel, 1963). According to Marzano (2007), "of vital importance to the success of critical input experiences is the extent to which the teacher organizes the experiences into small chunks" (p. 34).

Chunking also allows educators to examine the manner in which students experience new information (Marzano, 2007). When students are presented with new information, it is essential that the explanation is clear and not convoluted with simple language and that only the essence of the concept is presented without too many superfluous details. Then, students need time to recode or summarize the information in their own words either by writing the definition (or drawing a picture for younger children) or by communicating the definition to a partner. You could then circulate around the classroom to ensure that the information they write or communicate is accurate. For example, in an English class where students are learning about the different elements of narrative text writing, you may want to present each element—setting, characters, initiating event, complication, and solution—but the learning process would be far more effective if you presented each element using multiple formats (explanation, examples, and models) and stopped after each aspect, allowing students to process, either independently or with a partner, the unique aspects of each of the elements. If you are presenting information on rays, lines, and segments, you will likely be better off if you stop after each of these concepts or chunks, allowing students to process the definition and unique elements of each one.

In history, if students are learning about the various "isms" (communism, socialism, fascism, and so on), they will be well served if the teacher allows sufficient processing of each chunk prior to progressing to the next. For example, the concept of communism should be well processed prior to introducing students to the concept of socialism. Once each one has been processed in terms of its unique features, the next concept can be introduced.

Another critical reason for the effectiveness of chunking is to avoid fusing information that is similar (*socialism* and *communism*; *ray*, *line*, and *segment*; *river*, *lake*, *ocean*, and *sea*; *their*, *they're*, and *there*; *metaphor*, *analogy*, and *simile*) but needs to be recalled in terms of each of its unique elements (Marzano, 2007). This fusing of similar information occurs because our brains have learned to pattern information that is similar, a skill that is necessary because of the abundance of information that the brain needs to take in and process (Caine & Caine, 1991; Willis, 2007). When information is similar but needs to be recalled in terms of its unique features, it should be taught separately and chunked, with time allotted to process each of the chunks. Once students have processed the information, they can discuss the similarities and differences because they will have been provided with sufficient time to learn each topic as a separate entity.

THE PERILS OF TOO MANY SIMILAR CONCEPTS PRESENTED TOO QUICKLY WITHOUT CHUNKING

In an eighth-grade mathematics class, the teacher, who had years of experience teaching, presented the concept of ray, line, and segment within fifteen minutes of teaching. It became evident when she quizzed the students that each of these topics had been fused into one concept. Experienced teachers often remark that they teach in chunks, but upon closer reflection, it often becomes apparent that fusing occurs because of the lack of chunking, or slowing down the pace of instruction to teach one concept at a time.

RECODING

Recoding requires that students ponder what they have just learned and organize the information in a way that allows them to integrate this newly learned information within their overall schema (Lindley, 1966; Liu, Grady, & Moscovitch, 2018; Marks & Olson, 1981; Mayzner & Gabriel, 1963; van Kesteren, Krabbendam, & Meeter, 2018). This is best done through summarizing the content with key points, either on their own or with a partner; writing out the steps in a procedure; or creating a visual representation of the material. In some classes, especially with older students, they can do this in writing, but with younger students, if writing is still difficult for them, it is best if you ask them to respond orally to a partner. The key here is that they rephrase the information in their own words, creating symbolic representation of the information and processing it (Choy & Cheah, 2009; Lindley, 1966). Together, chunking and then recoding the learning is a powerhouse combination to ensure that what you teach sticks.

There's an intuitiveness to knowing how much to chunk and how often to allow for recoding. The more students know about the information, the larger the chunks or segments can become before recoding occurs; and the less they know about the information, the smaller the chunks should be. Recoding too often is like eating a steak in such tiny pieces that it can't be enjoyed, and talking for too long without recoding is like trying to bite off a chewy chunk of steak that's just too big to bite through (Marzano Center, 2012). In my capacity as an educational consultant, I have met with many teachers who worry that if they stop periodically for students to process new information, they won't have the time they need to "complete the chapter." What becomes abundantly clear, though, is that when we don't take the time to build recoding opportunities into each lesson for students to process newly learned information, then it is likely that *more* time will be required, not *less*, because we will inevitably need to repeat concepts that have not been mastered or reteach concepts that have been fused. Students must have sufficient processing time in order for new information to be digested, therefore requiring teachers to frequently pause (Bachhel & Thaman, 2014; Hattie, 2003; Porath, 2014; Rowe, 1986; Wood, 2002). Students can take notes during the teacher's presentation, but this still doesn't replace the need for recoding (Lindley, 1966; Marks & Olson, 1981; Mayzner & Gabriel, 1963).

WHY RECODING IS ESSENTIAL

In a grade 7 mathematics class, the teacher was going to miss two days of school because she was accompanying her eleventh-grade students on a school trip. The day before she left, she taught all of the steps in creating a factor tree. The students had learned this in elementary school, but very superficially, and many did not remember how to create one. She mentioned that she would teach all the steps, and that they would then perform the application of all steps with the substitute teacher during the two days she would be away.

Upon her return, she needed to go back to the very beginning because the students confused steps, were unsure about what to do, and felt frustrated and disappointed in their inability to complete the assignment. Not only did she need to reteach, this time one step at a time, but it

continued →

actually took longer because she needed to clear up misunderstandings and confusions that students had developed. After this experience, the teacher was able to reflect on the importance of slowing down, chunking material, and allowing time for students to recode and apply the information, one step at a time.

The different elements that teachers identify in their learning goals in terms of what students need to know by the end of the lesson can dictate when to pause and recode, and I would encourage you to revisit your learning goals until it becomes second nature to you. The implementation of recoding is challenging not because of an inherent difficulty in the strategy but rather from teachers thinking in too sophisticated a manner regarding its implementation. It helps to think of the strategies from the vantage point of the students. Will it likely be clear to them? If not, slow down and allow time for recoding.

Moving students from surface or new knowledge requires teachers to use strategies from stage 2, which focuses on consolidation and automaticity. These strategies will be discussed in the following section.

Stage 2: Consolidation and Automaticity

Vince Lombardi, the American football player and coach, coined the phrase "Practice does not make perfect. Only perfect practice makes perfect" (24/7 Sports, n.d.). And according to American poet Sarah Kay, practice makes permanent, for good or for bad (Kay, 2016).

The proficient development of skills requires a gradual release of responsibility that follows an "I do, we do, you do one, you do many" method. This step in the process is referred to as *consolidation*, where the students practice many examples to develop automaticity (Fisher & Frey, 2008; Levy, 2007; McCoy, 2011). Students need lots of practice for the skill to become automatic, and it is important to bear in mind that for ultimate proficiency, the practice needs to be accurate. For example, if a tennis player was determined to improve her game, she would need to identify the area in need of improvement, learn from an expert, and then engage in deliberative practice, highlighting the area to be worked on and ensuring that the practice is accurate. If a tennis player practiced ineffectively for hours, she would get much better at playing poorly.

New knowledge needs to be applied, and applied in the form of a skill, before it is lost. David Sousa (2006) presents the important steps required for effective practice that leads to proficient skill acquisition. Teachers should begin by presenting a small example. The application of that example should be modeled using a step-by-step process. The practice should take place over a short amount of time, during the lesson plan, while the student is focused on skill acquisition. The student should then practice the skill with just-in-time feedback whereby the teacher provides students with guided feedback immediately after they've engaged in the skill. The feedback is beneficial because it is is quick and specific (Brame & Director, 2018).

The memory demands on students are great. Students are bombarded with new information to consolidate all day long and in multiple topic areas. In addition, they're expected to learn and demonstrate the mastery of this knowledge regularly. How can educators facilitate the consolidation, memory, and automaticity of all this new knowledge we're asking them to absorb?

Let's use a mathematics example—how to find the area of a square. You could begin by giving the problem an authentic context, such as needing to measure the space in your house in order to purchase the correct number of tiles. Next, you could do a problem on the board while thinking out loud and ensuring that the students are paying attention, not writing, and without open laptops to distract them—just watching and listening. You articulate each step in the process: "First you need to . . . , then you need to . . . ." This is referred to as the "I do" phase of skill development. Rather than teaching students what we know, we are focusing on communicating to our students how we think and process information. Through this think-aloud process, you model for the students how to effectively and methodically solve a problem.

Next, take another example and have everyone do it together. In this "we do" phase in the process, we want students to mimic what we did previously with a second example, out loud and all at the same time. Most important, the students need to articulate the procedure, including the phrasing: "First we need to . . . , then we need to . . . ." The students' articulation of the steps in the process, as modeled by the teacher moments earlier, is essential for the development of strategic learners (Archer & Hughes, 2010; Biggs, 1996, 1999). To develop a strategy, students need to be intentional, purposeful, and metacognitive—hence, they must think of the procedure in terms of a series of steps, which they demonstrate through their phrasing. This is essential feedback that you must receive from your students. Even though they are responding together, it is fairly easy to identify, by scanning the class, if students appear to not know the steps.

The third step in the process is the "you do one" phase. At this point, everyone needs to complete one example independently, showing the steps in the process. While students are working, you can circulate and check their work. This phase can begin with students co-constructing their understanding, but each one will need to complete his or her own example to show evidence of initial mastery. Most will have done it accurately, so the consolidation or automaticity phase will begin (Reid, 2008). However, those who struggle will receive additional support from you, the teacher. The importance of each student completing one example prior to completing many relates to the "practice makes permanent" idea. If students do many problems before you can ensure that they have done one correctly, they will get very good at doing the exercises incorrectly (Fisher & Frey, 2008; Levy, 2007; McCoy, 2011). Therefore, this formative assessment phase of "you do one correctly before doing many" is essential.

The "you do many" phase is where students develop automaticity. They will need a lot of practice so that the skill becomes consolidated and they are able to move on to more sophisticated examples without having to expend too much energy on the skill. The brain resists having to work too hard because energy must be conserved for other, more demanding, tasks (De Jong, 2010; Sweller, 1994, 2011). Once students become proficient with regard to the skill, their energy is freed up to engage in higher-level and more sophisticated tasks (Dreyfus & Dreyfus, 1980; Sweller, 2011; van Merriënboer & Ayres, 2005).

This consolidation phase in the learning process, where surface learning is transitioning to deep learning, requires the teaching of not only context-specific strategies but also contextwide strategies such as note-taking, comprehension, and synthesizing information (De Jong, 2010; Goswami, 2008; Sweller, 2011). Again, you will need to teach these strategies explicitly, and the student must learn how to apply them in multiple contexts. I remember a university student who mentioned that she remembered her eighth-grade teacher with great fondness. Why this teacher? He taught her how to write an essay in the most methodical way. Every time she needs to write, she hears his voice. What a gift he gave her.

The following is an example of how you might apply the process of "I do, we do, you do one, you do many" in your classroom.

1. You begin by asking all students to close their computers, put down their pencils, and look at the board. This will likely take a few minutes as students may need to be asked a few times. It is such a critical stage in the process that it is worth looking at each student to make sure all are focused and looking at the board.

2. **I do**: You then begin the modeling by going through the steps and talking out loud. For example, you might say, *The first thing I need to do is to underline all like terms, each one in a different color. Hmmm, what is a like term? I will go to my definition. Here it states that like terms are . . . .*

The second thing I need to do is ask myself if I need to add or subtract each of the terms. I have to remember to keep the symbol in front of each term. I also have to remember that the symbol in front of the bracket affects all elements within the bracket. The third thing I need to do is to calculate the like terms.

3. **We do**: Using a slightly different example, all students complete the problem, clearly stating the steps in unison. All of the students would need to say: *First . . . . Second . . . . Third . . . .*

4. **You do one**: The students then individually complete another example that is, again, just slightly different than the other two. For example, $8x^2$ instead of $6x^2$, or $+3x - 4$ instead of $4x + 3$. At this point, you circulate around the classroom observing students completing the problem and making sure that they follow each of the steps. As they complete the problem, they need to write each of the steps on their papers as they work through the problem.

5. **You do many**: The students who completed the one problem correctly complete many. Those who struggled to complete the one problem work in a small group with the teacher to learn the skill correctly.

This process of consolidation must be supplemented by scaffolding to ensure the different needs of students in the class are adequately met. The term *scaffolding* refers to a process in which teachers model or demonstrate how to solve a problem, and then step back, offering support as needed (Hogan & Pressley, 1997; Pea, 2004; van de Pol et al., 2010), much like the scaffolding in architecture whereby the teacher is the scaffold and the student is the building. A scaffold functions to stabilize a building that is undergoing construction. At the start of the construction, the scaffold is holding up the building. Without the scaffold, the structure will not sustain itself. As the building strengthens, the scaffold is gradually reduced. Eventually, the scaffold is completely removed. As the student consolidates more and more new knowledge and skill, the educator—or scaffold—gradually relinquishes support commensurate with the student's capabilities. The master teacher is defined by this ability to be sensitive to the level of support required by the student and release control as required so that throughout the learning process, the student feels capable and has an "I can do it" attitude.

It is fascinating to see a master teacher in action. These teachers intuitively, but through practice, have learned when to provide a lot of support and when to release the level of support and encourage independence. With the strong support of the educator in the initial stage of skill development, learners feel as though they're in capable hands and as though they're able to follow the process with confidence.

This process of "I do, we do, you do one, you do many" is a perfect example of scaffolding. Scaffolding, which is based on Lev Vygotsky's (1978) *zone of proximal development*, occurs through the effective role modeling of the teacher and the gradual release of responsibility. The ZPD is defined as "the distance between the actual developmental level as determined by independent problem solving and the level of potential development as determined through problem solving under adult guidance, or in collaboration with more capable peers" (Vygotsky, 1978, p. 86). With regard to consolidation and skill implementation, the learning has to be in the students' ZPD. The vital question then becomes how to move the student from one who depends entirely on the educator to one who can independently problem solve, because if the task is too easy, you lose the student; if it's too hard, the student can't do it. Many teachers seem to believe that an overly difficult challenge will motivate students to work hard. I can recall many teachers saying that they enjoy presenting students with a challenge at the start of a new unit of study that they know is likely beyond the students' capability. Much research posits just the opposite is more effective (Chaiklin, 2003; Cheeseman, Clarke, Roche, & Walker, 2016; Doolittle, 1997; Moll, 1992; Roche & Clarke, 2014; Vygotsky, 1978). Initially, the teacher maintains primary responsibility, relinquishing control to the students very gradually and teaching them to gradually take on increasing independence (Fisher & Frey, 2008; E. Levy, 2007; McCoy, 2011).

It's certainly not always easy to know what is the right amount of support to give, nor is it easy to decide when and how to gradually release the support. Master educators are those who have developed a keen awareness of how much support to provide and when to reduce their support in relation to the student's capacity. This allows students to experience greater self-efficacy at the right time for them. It's not something you would expect yourself to know how to do in the early years of your career; however, it is an important skill to sharpen because it frees students to take ownership of their learning. Teachers are the backbone of a student's educational experience and development—the ones to give students everything they need to become independent so that as they get stronger, the scaffolding can come down (Fisher & Frey, 2008; Levy, 2007; van de Pol et al., 2010; Vygotsky, 1978).

Let's now go back to our example of calculating algebraic problems. The teacher would begin with an example on the board, such as $6x^2 - 4x + 3 - (2x^2 - 3x - 6)$ = ? She would teach the students how to complete the example by doing it on the board, explicitly listing each of the steps. If you were to enter the classroom, you might hear her say, "The first step is . . . . The second step is . . . . The third step is . . . ." This is the "I do" stage in the process. She would then perform the "we do" step by writing a second similar example on the board and having all students state the steps in unison. She would pay attention to whether all students were speaking and stating one step of the process at a time. For the "you do one" step, students would then complete a similar example by themselves. Those students who correctly completed the example would then do many so that the process becomes consolidated or automatic. Those students who incorrectly completed the example would work with the teacher on numerous examples, going back to the steps required to complete the example.

Once the learning is consolidated and automatic, students must discover how to apply this learning to novel circumstances. This is explained in Stage 3: Transfer.

Stage 3: Transfer

Once the students have solidified the skill—meaning they can perform it quickly and accurately—they are ready for more sophisticated tasks, because the skill required to engage in the initial task does not require as much concentration or focus (Collins et al., 1991; Collins, Brown, & Newman, 1989; Fisher et al., 2016; van Merriënboer & Sweller, 2005). The student is becoming an expert and is ready for new tasks that need to neither closely resemble those already mastered nor follow a script, template, or structure as in surface learning. Group work is most effective here because the students can challenge one another, build on one another's knowledge, create new associations, and apply it to new contexts (Hattie, 2008, 2012; McDowell, 2020). According to Bloom's revised taxonomy (Anderson et al., 2001), the learner is now able to create new products and performances that are based on the knowledge and skills that were learned but are authentic and purposeful. The student can now begin to think like a historian, scientist, journalist, or any other professional, and solve real-world problems. Students can now create what only exists in their own minds—but with the application of the knowledge and skills they learned throughout the unit. This is known as *transfer*.

Learning begins as a slow, explicit, teacher-controlled, and purposeful activity. However, as the student gains knowledge, skill acquisition, and confidence, he or she can begin to engage in sophisticated tasks that are more student-driven and less teacher-controlled, and that require more creative outputs. For example, in the beginning of a unit on fractions, teachers go through lots of modeling with the students, after first explaining the concept: how to do mathematical equations with fractions. After the teacher does one example—let's say ¾ − ½ = ¼— the whole class does one together. Following the "I do one, we do one, you do one, you do many" strategy as the teacher, we slowly decrease our modeling and our scaffolding with the students as they increasingly understand the concept of fractions. Finally, after many correct examples, these experts can then attempt more creative outputs, such as using their knowledge in fractions to plan a party for a classmate with food and loot bags. Throughout the process, the teacher can seek student input through more formalized formative assessment as well as quick check-ins (for example, "How are you doing? How are you feeling about this? Do you have any questions?") throughout the learning process. Teachers should encourage students to ask questions, because students' questions are often a window into how they are thinking.

Imagine a student of yours today and envision him or her in fifteen or twenty years. Ultimately, you would want to know whether he or she learned what you taught and whether that remained as he or she went off into the world. Ask yourself what you can do in your role as an educator, with the tools, resources, and knowledge you have, that will prepare that child for the future. It is my hope that educators will access and use everything available to them to ensure that their vision for their students is realized and, even more, that teachers remain excited about the difference they make when it's reflected back to them by the success of the kids they taught.

The teaching and learning process this chapter describes, along with corresponding strategies, can be seen in the reproducible "Strategies and Examples to Incorporate Strategic Teaching and Learning" on page 63. You can print your own blank version of this chart at **go.SolutionTree.com/instruction** to record your own ideas.

⌐ NEXT STEPS

Try out the new structure shown in the reproducible "Teaching Process Template for the Three Stages of Teaching and Learning" (page 65) with your students. Begin by identifying your learning goals for a lesson or a few lessons. Then start with new knowledge: what students need to know, understand, and be able to do by the end of the lesson. (These steps were discussed in more detail in chapter 2, page 25.) Remember to stop periodically to allow students to recode the new information. Then move into consolidation and "I do, we do, you do one, you do many." During the "you do many" part of the learning process, students should work on their own so that each student develops mastery of the goal. Finally, have students work in pairs or small groups and challenge them with a complex problem as they become experts.

Strategies and Examples to Incorporate Strategic Teaching and Learning

STAGE IN THE TEACHING AND LEARNING PROCESS	STRATEGY	EXAMPLE
Stage 1: Surface or New Knowledge	Preassessment	Answer true or false science questions from a previous grade level or topic.
		Write a paragraph about an image and include figurative language.
		Complete a mathematics problem from the previous grade level or topic.
	Anchor activities	Provide challenging examples for students who have mastered the prerequisite skills (as evidenced by the preassessment), such as the following: write a paragraph using four examples of hyperbole, complete complex mathematics problems, write mathematics problems.
	Explicit teaching	Use a reliable source when teaching new material (for example, a textbook, a reliable internet source, or a teacher lecture).
		Name strategies as you teach them (for example, "I am now going to teach you a strategy called reciprocal teaching").
		Teach the steps involved in problem solving (for example, "The first step in reciprocal teaching is to look at the front cover of the text and predict what you think the text will be about").

Page 1 of 2

Stage 1: Surface or New Knowledge *(continued)*	Chunking material	Say, "First we are going to learn how to write the setting and characters in a narrative text. Here are some examples." Teach, "First we are going to learn about what a ray is." Say, "First we are going to learn about capitalism."
	Recoding	Stop after each chunk for students to summarize the concept or definition in their own words in writing or orally with a partner.
Stage 2: Consolidation and Automaticity	Modeling the steps	I do: Review one example using a think-aloud ("First you look for the brackets; then, once you find the brackets, you . . . .") We do: Show students another similar example. Everyone in the class completes the example in unison highlighting the steps. You do one: Each student completes one example in writing, highlighting the steps. You do many: Once students have been able to correctly complete one example, then they practice many.
	Scaffolding	Begin with an example that the students can complete successfully, and then gradually increase the difficulty.
Stage 3: Transfer	Applying the skill in an authentic context	Say, "Now that you have learned how to complete an algebraic example, calculate what the cost of our outing next week will be if 50 percent of the class attends, if 75 percent of the class attends, or if 100 percent of the class attends."

Page 2 of 2

Teaching Process Template for the Three Stages of Teaching and Learning

Learning Goals:		
K:		
U:		
D:		
STAGE	EXPLANATION	YOUR EXAMPLE
Stage 1: Surface or New Knowledge	What facts, vocabulary, or procedural knowledge (steps) do students need to master?	
Stage 2: Consolidation and Automaticity	I do: Write out the dialogue of your talk-aloud. We do: Write out your new but similar example and the correct answer or response. You do one: Write out a third but similar example. You do many: List the exercises you want your students to complete.	
Stage 3: Transfer	Now your students are becoming experts. Write out a challenging task that you can present to your students.	

Improving Classroom Management

The ability to manage a classroom is perhaps one of the greatest challenges of teaching (Baker, 2005). What strikes me most, each and every time I enter a classroom, is the way in which teachers present themselves to their students at the start of each class. It is apparent from the first moments of class whether or not students are learning. In classrooms where effective learning is occurring, teachers speak with conviction, are organized, and begin by making a connection with what was reviewed in the last lesson, in order to move students into the day's class. For example, they may begin by reminding students that in the last class they outlined the first three causes of World War II, or the steps involved in adding fractions with like denominators. They provide a quick review of these points and then introduce the learning goals for the day's lesson. Oftentimes, these learning goals will be written on the board. There's an aura in the room that this is a safe place and that all are going to learn. As the observer in the classroom, I feel it, and so do the students. It might seem like one of those intangibles in education, but it can be parsed into specific actions that occur, the clarity of instructions, and other elements essential to effective classroom management.

Of the many facets related to effective classroom management, in this chapter I will highlight three points that will have a major impact on creating a classroom that is conducive to learning (Gordon, 2001; Hulac & Briesch, 2017; Rockwell, 2006; Sieberer-Nagler, 2016):

1. Behavior problems are always a signal to the educator that something isn't right with the student. The question is, are we listening?

2. The only person who can change in the relationship between a student who is poorly behaved and the teacher interacting with him or her is the educator.

3. The concept of *withitness* has been touted as one of the most effective strategies witnessed by teachers, who are masters of classroom management (Gordon, 2001).

As always, the strategies related to these points will be presented, along with a plan for next steps to help you as you implement this principle in your classroom.

⚡ THE CHALLENGE

Poor behavior has a function, and that function is a form of communication (Pereira & Smith-Adcock, 2011). Behavior problems are often a signal that something isn't right with the student (Gleason, Goldson, Yogman, & Council on Early Childhood, 2016). Poor behavior is often the only form of communication that the student knows to inform an adult in his or her life that something is wrong (McEvoy & Welker, 2000). While many teachers simply see the poor behavior and resultant chaos, the actual problems go deeper than simply misbehavior. The most important thing to do to solve this problem is simply to *listen* for what the poor behavior is communicating. And once the behavior is understood, students need to learn a new set of behavioral skills that will help them achieve their goal (Weber, 2018).

Students cannot learn in a classroom that is not well managed. The result is a group of frustrated students and an equally frustrated and exhausted teacher. However, by keeping in mind some basic principles and practicing them, small improvements will become apparent. At the heart of effective management is the connection that you manage to establish with your students and specific tactics that enable both teacher and students to thrive.

There are many strategies that can be applied in the classroom that will support teachers in their overall classroom management. Most important to note is that classroom management is a *prerequisite* to classroom learning. Very limited learning can take place in a classroom that is poorly managed. However, effective teaching and learning strategies that include active engagement and clear learning goals are essential elements that lead to effective classroom management (Weber, 2018). Equally important, it is a mistake to believe that there is a divide between the novice and more experienced teacher with regard to overall management. Effective classroom management is challenging not only for the novice teacher but also for more experienced teachers. Throughout my years working with teachers, both novices and veteran teachers have expressed to me the exhaustion that they feel as a result of not being able to effectively manage their classroom.

✥ THE PRINCIPLE

The key to addressing poor behavior is to understand it first—understand what its function is and what purpose it serves (Little, 2020; OSEP Center on Positive Behavioral Interventions and Supports et al., 2000). The most effective way to do this is to pay attention to what seems to trigger the poor behavior. Since all behaviors serve a function, we need to pay close attention to what the student is telling us through his or her behavior. On the surface you see a misbehaving student, but if you stop and listen to what is really going on, you will see and hear a student who has too many stresses in his life; or a student with few, if any, friends; or a student who can't read; or a student who feels as though he has no control over his life. The result is poor behavior, but the message will almost always be apparent when you take the time to listen (Ayllon & Michael, 1959; Iwata et al., 2000; James, 2016; Maazouzi, 2017; McIntosh, Brown, & Borgmeier, 2008).

It is imperative that you examine the trigger for the poor behavior, because inevitably the student is trying to communicate a discomfort or need that, at that given time, can only be heard or responded to through misbehavior (McIntosh et al., 2008; Pereira & Smith-Adcock, 2011; Wolff, Jarodzka, & Boshuizen, 2017). Some common triggers are avoidance, attention seeking, and stimulation seeking.

A critical piece in understanding poor behavior is examining the consequences that ensue. If your student's misbehavior is a form of avoidance, and the result is that she is removed from the classroom, she succeeded in achieving her goal. If a student is looking for attention (either positive or negative), and you interrupt your classroom to focus on him, he gains the attention he seeks. If a student is seeking stimulation in the classroom, a passive, unengaging classroom that suddenly fills with tumult results in her needs being momentarily met.

As stated previously, it's important to note that poor behavior is a form of communication, that there is often a trigger for this misbehavior, and that the consequence reinforces the behavior (Cone, 1997; Durand, 1987; Johnston & Pennypacker, 1993; McIntosh et al., 2008). So, what should you do?

One thing is certain in creating a healthy classroom environment: punishment doesn't work. There is a plethora of research on the ineffectiveness of punishment (Cameron & Pierce, 1994; Hattie, 2012; Hattie & Timperley, 2007; Kelly & Pohl, 2018; Maag, 2001; Obi, 2020; Schmidt, 1982; Shults, Brock, Millay, & Keesey, 2019; Tauber, 1995). What happens when punishment is used? By punishing the behavior, the student is not learning what he or she is supposed to be doing appropriately but instead is learning that he or she should be doing the same punished behavior in a more covert, discreet way so as to hide it from the teacher. Hattie (2008) has shown that the least-effective feedback you can provide to students is punishment. Teachers who punish instill fear in their students (Myers, 1999), which can lead to a negative impact in their academic performance (Guthrow, 2002) and cause students to lose interest in the subject as students associate the fear and negative feelings not simply with the behavior, but with the teacher who enforced punishment. Hence, students become disinterested in class (Coon, 2001).

⊕ THE STRATEGY

To manage the classroom and avoid misbehavior, we need to focus on three different elements.

1. Alter the trigger.

2. Avoid reinforcement.

3. Teach appropriate ways to communicate.

In addition, you can utilize several other strategies to manage your classroom, including the following.

4. Establish rules and procedures.

5. Ensure students have necessary materials.

6. Address avoidance behaviors.

7. Divert attention seeking.

8. Provide appropriate opportunities for stimulation seeking.

9. Remember, the only behavior you can control is your own.

10. Use withitness to master classroom management.

11. Maintain positivity in the classroom.

12. Be prepared.

13. Provide clarity.

We will detail each of these in the following sections.

Alter the Trigger

Triggers, otherwise referred to as *antecedents*, are likely to be the cause of the student's misbehavior. When addressing misbehavior, it is important first to identify and subsequently try to alter the trigger for such behavior. For example, as mentioned previously, if the classwork is too difficult, and it is this difficult work that causes the student to misbehave, you could try to provide work that the student can successfully complete, or you could provide an accommodation. As will be discussed in chapter 5 (page 89), when planning lessons it is very useful to think about your students and identify if any of your students might have difficulty with the assigned classwork. Preassesment data (mentioned in chapter 3, page 43) can be very enlightening in terms of identifying which of your students are having difficulty with a particular skill or content knowledge. For these students, rather than having them work on the assigned task and subsequently fail, it would be useful to have an alternative, less challenging assigned task aligned with their current readiness level. You might want to try using a template for a student who is having difficulty writing a narrative text. The subheadings could be setting, characters, initiating event, complication, and resolution. You might ask the student to draw a picture for each element—a picture of the setting, characters, and so on. You could then direct the student to write a few words for each image. The student could then expand these few words to longer sentences and eventually paragraphs.

Another example of a trigger could be an overstimulating classroom, one that is either very noisy or visually overstimulating with too much affixed to the walls. It is essential that we recognize how difficult it is for students to attend to work in a noisy classroom, and therefore it's best to explain to students the challenges brought about when there is too much noise. As well, be aware of classrooms with too many visual displays on the walls. A few posters are good, but too many are problematic. By being aware of these issues, teachers can attempt to alter potential triggers.

AVOIDING OVERSTIMULATION IN THE CLASSROOM

A number of years ago, a teacher was struggling with the maladaptive behaviors of a grade 4 student on the autism spectrum. He would enter class and quickly become overwhelmed with the number of activities available to him. To avoid his sense of overstimulation, the teacher explained to the class that she would leave only a few toys on display. If there was some other activity that they wanted to play with, they would need to ask, and she would get it for them. A teacher in one of my graduate classes spoke of another example as a way to alter a disturbing trigger. A student in her class, also on the spectrum, would get very disturbed each time students would clap. To avoid this troubling situation, she asked her students to air clap without making any noise. What a wonderful way to engage all students in the support of one of their classmates.

Avoid Reinforcement

Second, you need to make sure not to reinforce the maladaptive behavior. This means you must look carefully at your own responses to student misbehavior. When you remove a misbehaving student from the classroom, he gains the escape he was hoping for. If you reprimand a student, you are giving her the attention she was seeking. When you let misbehavior escalate, you are providing the sensory stimulation that student is looking for. As mentioned earlier in this chapter, misbehavior is often a sign of the student needing something that he is not currently receiving. Typically, student misbehavior is a sign of the student seeking attention, avoidance, or stimulation. If the student finds the class understimulating (for example, a lecture that is going on for too long), his misbehavior might result in excitement in the classroom. He may perceive the reprimand as more "fun" than the lecture that was taking place. If the student is seeking attention, then being reprimanded is in essence providing the student with what he is looking for. Thus, reprimanding students will likely reinforce their poor behavior by giving them what they need—attention—even if it is through their misbehavior.

Teachers often express to me that they are perplexed about why their reprimands fail to result in a cessation of the misbehavior but instead lead to increased misbehavior. It is important to note that the reason the poor behavior persists is because the student wanted something—attention or stimulation—and his poor behavior gave him what he was seeking. Why, then, would the poor behavior cease (Osborne, 2019)?

Teach Appropriate Ways to Communicate

Next, and perhaps most important, you should try to teach students more adaptive ways of responding or communicating their needs. For example, you could try to guide them to ask for help if they are struggling with a mathematics problem or a writing task. If students need more stimulation, it's possible to have them leave the class for a few moments. For students who need less stimulation in a class that they find tumultuous, you might also give them the green light to leave the class for a few moments (Gage, Lewis, & Stichter, 2012).

Hold this idea close every time you're about to enter the classroom to teach your students: *nothing changes if nothing changes*. You, the purposeful teacher, are the agent of change in these scenarios. Once the misbehavior occurs, it's important that you ensure it's not being reinforced.

Establish Rules and Procedures

An important starting point at the beginning of the year is establishing rules and procedures. A rule sets the foundation for behaviors that are acceptable or unacceptable in the classroom. For example, one rule might be no use of bad language in the classroom, an important rule especially in the high school classroom. When students neglect to follow rules, they usually incur an associated consequence. Rather than provide consequences for students who don't follow rules, it is best to practice *procedures*—processes that students must follow for the smooth and effective running of the classroom—until the rules are mastered. Students may be reprimanded for calling out to a friend at the other side of the classroom, but if the procedures are clear—such as by having the teacher always assigning the groups—students are less likely to be reprimanded. You can try to list the procedures involved in dividing students into groups. These may involve steps such as looking on the board for your groups, moving to your groups on the count of three, taking your chair but not your desk, and beginning the assignment as listed on the task sheet. If the procedure is clear, and students have sufficient practice with reinforcement when they follow the procedure, they will be more likely to avoid actions leading to reprimands (Alter & Haydon, 2017).

Ensure Students Have Necessary Materials

Students coming to class without the necessary materials often leads to behavioral disruptions because these students cannot do their work. When work is assigned, rather than hearing students beginning their work, you'll hear a cacophony of students inform you that they don't have their materials. This is hard to manage in any classroom. Therefore, greeting students at the door to ensure they have their materials is an important way to begin each class and helpful for classroom management—especially in high school classrooms, where students are more likely to move from class to class. If students forget their materials, you may decide to either let students get their materials from their locker or provide them with an extra set of materials. In addition, you many decide to provide a consequence as per your school's policy. However, to avoid chaos in the classroom it is best to ensure that all students have the needed materials. I strongly recommend having an extra set of materials, especially for the students who have multiple challenges such as learning issues, behavioral or social challenges, or family issues. There are only so many issues that can be addressed at one time, and not having the materials pales in comparison to the other, more significant issues.

Setting clear learning goals for the lesson provides students with the information that they need to prepare themselves for what they are going to learn. Also, while you are preparing yourself to get started, take attendance, or organize your materials, a challenging question on the board for all students to respond to will provide structure as soon as they enter.

Address Avoidance Behaviors

Misbehavior can be a signal that a student needs or wants to escape. Students may misbehave in order to get kicked out of the classroom so that they won't have to complete the assigned work (Barbetta, Norona, & Bicard, 2005; Pereira & Smith-Adcock, 2011). For example, imagine that you have just instructed the students to find a partner and begin reading a segment of text. A student who struggles to read might try to get kicked out of class for fear that his or her learning disability will become known to his or her peers. In these situations, and in line with being purposeful in our teaching, it is essential to think about what we want students to learn and which of our students might struggle to gain access to the learning. Thinking about these points in a purposeful way will enable you to ascertain, in the planning of your lesson, if there are students who will likely struggle to achieve any of the goals you've identified. Addressing the potential barriers to students' learning prior to beginning the teaching will reduce the likelihood that students will misbehave in order to avoid doing their work (Martinez, Mcmahon, Coker, & Keys, 2016).

Divert Attention Seeking

A student who feels that he has limited control over his life will try multiple ways of gaining attention (Pereira & Smith-Adcock, 2011; Marzano & Marzano, 2001). Students who feel they're not getting the attention they need from peers or the teacher may also use inappropriate behaviors to attract attention (Barbetta et al., 2005). They may seek attention because they feel excluded or isolated. The exact reason may be less important in the context of the classroom, but the need for attention is clear. A student who calls out, acts silly, or tries out for the part of class clown is exactly that student.

For students who seek attention, try to provide them with the attention they are seeking *before* they need to act out in order to get it. For example, find out what interests them and ask them questions about it at the start of class whenever possible (for example, "How was your hockey game last night? Did your parents return from their holiday? How's your little sister doing?"). Many students who seek attention need the teacher to notice them—to have someone affirm to them that they're seen, that the teacher notices they are here. Offer these students this affirmation by acknowledging their presence at the start of each class.

As teachers, we can help students who seek attention by providing appropriate ways for them to get it. If a student has no friends, address this critical social problem in the class. Arrange partners for students; find the kindest student in the class and have him or her partner with the student at first. Model a classroom that is safe and welcoming; students follow what they see. Talk to students about the importance of inclusion, and work with this student to help him or her find more appropriate behaviors, if necessary.

You might also provide the student with a leadership role whenever possible or try fabricating opportunities for him or her to help, such as having the student get needed class material (paper or a stapler). Students who crave attention often enjoy the positive attention they get from helping and thrive in leadership positions because, again, they are receiving attention from others.

Try teaching replacement behaviors. For example, you might say, "When you need my attention, give me a sign such as raising your hand or putting your pencil down in a certain way." You can tell your students, "When I see the sign, I'll know you need me, and I'll do my best to come to you as soon as I can." Then, teach them some appropriate behaviors they can use. When they approximate appropriate behavior, be sure to encourage them each and every time.

HELP ME; I DON'T UNDERSTAND WHAT TO DO

In one particular classroom, a student erupted in cawing noises when the teacher began distributing a worksheet based on the reading they had done the previous day that was to be completed in class. When the teacher approached, he yelled, "This is so dumb! I'm not doing this work." He was immediately sent out of class and instructed to meet with the principal. He didn't offer any information, but when asked what happened, he said, in the same belligerent tone he had used in class, "I have no clue what the story is about. How can I answer questions?" The tactic was clear. He was communicating with the teacher, albeit in a maladaptive way, that he was unable to complete the work.

A possible solution for a student who doesn't understand the learning might be to begin the class with a summary of the previous day's work. A formative assessment (to be discussed in chapter 5, page 89) is an excellent way to identify if the students have met the learning goals for each class. A question or two at the end of class might indicate that one or more of your students have not mastered the goals. This information can be useful as you plan for the remainder of the class or the next class. At the start of class, you might want to provide those students who have mastered the material, as evident from the formative assessment, a few review questions to respond to, while you spend a few minutes with those students who have not mastered the goals. If you are concerned that this might single out some students and that they wouldn't respond well to this, the class lesson can begin with a clear summary of the previous day highlighting those points that were unclear, again as evident in the formative assessment. For example, if students need to have a clear understanding of the events in a story and this poses a challenge for some students (perhaps the story is in a language that is not the students' first language), you can begin with a slideshow with pictures and a few key words highlighting the main ideas in the story.

THE IMPORTANCE OF STARTING A LESSON WITH A REVIEW OF THE PREVIOUS CLASS

In one classroom I observed, the teacher asked students a few key questions at the end of class pertaining to a story that they had read. It was clear that some students had missed some very important information and had not mastered the key vocabulary they needed to understand the story. She began the next day's lesson with a slideshow with an image on each slide with key words below the image. The image was vital in ensuring that those few students knew the main events in the story along with those key words. The students' faces showed relief; their teacher had provided an unobtrusive review tailored to their needs that allowed them to understand.

Provide Appropriate Opportunities for Stimulation Seeking

The student who seeks sensory stimulation may be a student who has been labeled with attention deficit hyperactivity disorder (ADHD; Kos, Richdale, & Hay, 2006). In a class with limited engagement, this student might respond impulsively, seeking sensory stimulation (Barbetta et al., 2005). His impulsive act (he might have just thrust a pen into his classmate's shoulder) results in exactly what he was looking for—action in the classroom. Suddenly, this passive classroom setting is now filled with action.

In all classrooms, students benefit from the opportunity to remain engaged throughout the class. *Classroom centers* provide valuable ways for students to work in smaller groups engaged in a particular activity to develop a goal (Wilson, 2016). For example, in an English language arts class, after teaching the skill of sentence writing, each center could highlight a different aspect of writing. In one center, students could be shown a picture and asked to write a few expository sentences about that picture. In another center, students could be given prompts and asked to complete the sentence. In yet another center, students could be given plasticized words and asked to put them in the correct order to make a complete sentence. In a fourth center, students could be using computer programs such as Grammar Jammers, Sentence Builder, Grammar Pop, or Little Bird Tales to develop sentence and story writing. Finally, in a fifth center, students could be asked to use computer programs such as Verb Crash to correct incorrect sentences.

A SIMPLE STRATEGY FOR A STUDENT WHO NEEDS ADDITIONAL STIMULATION TO FOCUS

I once witnessed an interesting strategy that a high school teacher used to provide additional sensory stimulation for a restless student who was disturbing the class. The teacher asked this student to stand at the back of the class on one foot. As odd as this sounds, it worked. The need to focus on balancing on one foot is just what this student needed in order to focus and pay attention. In another class, a teacher brought in her ironing board to class to serve as a stand-up desk for those who needed one. She suggested that a few students, who were having difficulty remaining in their seats, go to the back of the class and stand while using the board as their desk. The only thing she required of them was to remain within arm's length of the board. They happily went to the back and were able to remain on task because they were given the green light to stand rather than remain seated at the desks.

Remember, the Only Behavior You Can Control Is Your Own

This ties nicely into the next point. The only behavior that you can control is your own. Over the years, I have heard teachers lament the fact that student behaviors are out of control—and they need to be controlled! Ultimately, however, the only behavior we can control is our own (Rockwell, 2006).

COMMUNICATION TAKES MANY FORMS

Some years ago, I was observing a high school classroom. A student who had many challenges, mostly in the area of behavior, was sitting atop his desk at the back of the classroom while all the other students were at their desks completing a writing assignment. He then moved from this desk to another desk in the front of the classroom. This continued for a few minutes. He would try to catch the teacher's gaze and then move to another spot in the classroom and sit on the desk. The teacher was becoming increasingly frustrated as she was trying to help other students while at the same time trying to figure out how to respond to this one student. A few moments later, she lost it and screamed, "If you don't sit down immediately, you'll be sent to the office!" As could be predicted, he continued, partly for my benefit, and was sent to the office. The next day, he returned to class and tried this again, with the same result. We can't force or make students behave, and we can't physically control them—nor should we even try. The only behavior we can control is our own. In almost all cases (except perhaps in the case of students who have oppositional behavior), student behaviors will improve when we learn to manage our own.

In this case, after a short conversation with the teacher, there was an understanding of this important principle. I asked her what she wanted. Her response was, of course, to have the student work on the task at his desk. What could she do to make this happen? We talked about the fact that when agitated, it is very difficult to think clearly. She needed to remain calm and think about what she could say to the student. She began by encouraging him. Rather than call out or disrupt others, the student was moving from desk to desk, perhaps as a way to remain calm. She rewarded him for this. She then asked if he needed any help to get the assignment completed. In this case, he was capable of completing the task, but needed to make a connection with the teacher. She allowed this

continued →

to happen by approaching him at the start of the next class, asking him where he wanted to sit, and telling him that he could sit on the desk if this made it easier for him to work—even if it was somewhat disruptive to others. She let him know that she would be looking his way often in case he needed some help. The student seemed to calm down immediately. He remained on the desk the next class, but at the start of the following class, he returned to his own seat.

Sylvia Rockwell (2006), in her book *You Can't Make Me!*, writes that our job as educators is not to force students into compliance but to teach them how to be responsible and how to control their own behaviors. The only way to do this is when we come to the realization that the only behavior that we can control is our own. Therefore, we need to take a deep breath and practice how to manage ourselves. We need to think about how we can respond from a position of calmness and consistency instead of anger or frustration. Reactive responses perpetuate the negative activity, but once we learn to manage our own selves, most students will step up and respond favorably (Sutton, Mudrey-Camino, & Knight, 2009).

Use Withitness to Master Classroom Management

Withitness means having eyes in the back of your head (Brophy, 1986; Kounin, 1970; Wolff, Jarodzka, van den Bogert, & Boshuizen, 2016). When thinking of the teacher who lacks withitness, what comes to mind is the teacher writing on the blackboard, unaware of what is transpiring behind him or her. The most effective teachers engage individually with students, providing support, while also keeping an eye on the other students in the classroom (Brophy, 1986; Kunter, Baumert, & Köller, 2007)—not an easy task, but one that is essential and that sends the message to students that you are aware of what is going on.

Students need to know that you are present both physically and instructionally, ready and able to provide guidance as needed. Having withitness means that you can engage individually with students but never at the expense of losing the ability to engage with others when and if needed. It therefore also involves positioning yourself in the classroom so that you are able to see all students, so that you can respond to misbehaviors quickly and effectively and reinforce behaviors that deserve to be reinforced.

Teachers who are *with it* are also measured in their responses, partly because they are able to respond quickly and effectively but also because they have a sense of the appropriate level of response that they need to address a problem.

The response is appropriate to the situation, such as a quiet reminder to remain on task or to engage with others in a more adaptive manner. Witit teachers do this without breaking the flow of the classroom. When a student is off task or is showing early signs of maladaptive behaviors, beginning with simply redirecting the student helps to maintain the flow of the lesson. Redirecting can take the form of removing a marker from a student's hand if you see it is about to be propelled across the classroom. No engagement with the student is necessary beyond removing the marker.

One strategy to support withitness in the classroom is the placement of students. Those students who need more attention from the teacher could be placed in one section of the class, preferably close to the front of the room. This will make it easier to have quick access to these students. Also, quick physical access to all students is essential; therefore, you should arrange desks so that you can walk freely around the class engaging with individuals or groups of students throughout the lesson. Proximity is key here—it is best to walk around the classroom while teaching rather than remain at the front.

Technology can aid in this regard significantly. When you are presenting material to students—for example, the various systems of the body (circulatory, digestive, and so on)—using a laptop to write notes on the board while circulating around the classroom is an excellent idea. You can both present new material on the board and engage with individual students. This is not an easy task, but a very useful one to maintain withitness while you teach. Another strategy, which sounds simple but is not always evident, is how you place yourself when you speak with students. It is important to avoid facing some students while putting your back to the remaining students in the class. Preferably, stand in back of the student facing the classroom whenever possible.

Maintain Positivity in the Classroom

Maintaining a positive classroom environment is another essential element of effective management (Martin, Linfoot, & Stephenson, 1999). "Catching students being good" is a useful phrase because it reminds us that students are more likely to show us the behaviors that we pay attention to, highlight, and reinforce (Conroy & Sutherland, 2012). It's not uncommon for a teacher who struggles with classroom management to get lost in a mire of negativity. I have spent a lot of time in these classrooms, and comments such as "Stop that," "Would you like it if . . . ," "Start doing your work," "Get back to your seat," and "Raise your hand before you speak" constitute the common banter. This eventually becomes white noise, and students in this environment will continue to present maladaptive behaviors, creating a loop of negativity (Pereira & Smith-Adcock, 2011; Spilt, Leflot, Onghena, & Colpin, 2016) that will take its toll on everyone in the class, including you. What if we were to reframe how we speak to promote these proactive behaviors? For example, to the student who has trouble sitting, instead of "Get back to your seat," we need to catch him or her seated and say, "Awesome, Richard, you're in your seat. Thank you." Or, instead of "Start doing your work," how about catching someone who's usually slow to start and saying, "Look at you, Nikki, you've got a good start there!"

One of the most effective ways of shifting from a classroom full of negative talk to a positive classroom environment is to think of presenting four positive comments for every negative comment (Trussell, 2008). This 4:1 ratio is critical to turn a negative classroom environment to a positive one and enables students to begin to present the behaviors that they hear so often being reinforced by the teacher (Trussell, 2008). Redirection is also considered a negative comment (Soleman, Ata, & Salah, 2019; Umbreit, 1996). If you need to remind a student to focus on the task at hand, the comment is perceived as negative rather than positive. For every redirection or negative comment such as "You need to raise your hand before you speak," "Get back to your seat," or "Start working on the assignment," students need to hear four positive comments such as "You're putting a lot of effort into the assignment," "You're all working very nicely in your group," and "You used an excellent strategy to solve the equation." The positive comment does not need to be directed at the same student who received the negative comment. Rather, the goal is to fill the classroom with four times as many positive comments as negative comments (Trussell, 2008).

THE 4:1 RATIO OF POSITIVE TO NEGATIVE COMMENTS

In one of my undergraduate classes, the students committed to attempting this 4:1 ratio in their own classrooms. After trying it, each one reported that it sounded easier to do than it really was. We are far more likely to focus on what we don't want to see rather than the behaviors that should be reinforced (Shores et al., 1993). Nonetheless, they kept working on it. Each week, they would report on the progress of this strategy. Two months later, all of the students remarked that with perseverance and steadfastness, they were able to turn the negative classroom environment into a more positive one. They began to witness students whose negative behaviors had become their default gradually engaging in the behaviors that were being so frequently reinforced. Transitioning from a negative environment, where students hear the word *don't* more frequently than any other word, to an environment that highlights the positive behaviors is not simple to do, but with practice, it eventually becomes a natural part of the classroom vernacular.

By reframing and redirecting our negative comments to more positive ones, we will have great influence over students' ability to focus, attend, and learn (Noble & McGrath, 2008). Theodore Roosevelt's powerful and timeless quote, "No one cares how much you know until they know how much you care" (Theodore Roosevelt Center, n.d.), is as true today as it was when he said it at the turn of the 20th century. At the heart of it all are the connections that we establish with our students. When we learn the tactics that will support student learning through the management of our own behaviors, we can build strong and meaningful connections with our students (Jennings & Greenberg, 2009; Marzano & Marzano, 2001).

Be Prepared

Of course, positivity alone is not enough. Preparedness is an essential element of a positive and well-run classroom.

THE IMPORTANCE OF COMING TO CLASS PREPARED

A number of years ago, I was invited to spend a few days in a school to work with teachers struggling with classroom management. One of the first teachers I worked with was a high school teacher who was unable, as she said, to "gain control of the classroom." I entered the class a few moments before the students. The students entered one by one or in small groups and sat down waiting for the class to begin. The teacher was visibly unprepared. There was a story she wanted them to read, but the questions they needed to answer were not readily available. Her class

continued →

immediately erupted in chaos with students talking to one another and moving around the classroom. They saw that she was preoccupied with finding the page number and therefore decided to use the spare time as an opportunity to disrupt.

One thing is for certain: it's necessary to be prepared for class in order to ensure effective classroom management (Giallo & Little, 2003; Martella, Nelson, & Marchand-Martella, 2003; Marzano & Marzano, 2001). Being purposeful in teaching involves thinking about the rollout of all lessons. My advice to you is to imagine that the lesson is like a film with individual scenes. Think of what materials will be needed for each scene, and make sure they're readily available. At times, it can be overwhelming to think of the needs for a full period, especially longer periods of sixty or seventy-five minutes. Breaking the lesson into blocks or scenes makes it more manageable to ensure the planning is done and the materials are easily accessible. Coming to class prepared and ready to teach also minimizes non-instructional time. These downtimes during the lesson, when students are off task and not engaged in work, can lead to disruptions, so do your best to avoid them.

Provide Clarity

Clarity is another essential element of effective classroom management. Often, behavior deteriorates because of a lack of teacher clarity (Chesebro & McCroskey, 2001). When students are unsure or confused about what is expected of them, the result is confusion, frustration, and often chaos (Alter & Haydon, 2017; Mahvar, Farahani, & Aryankhesa, 2018; Marzano & Marzano, 2001; Nussbaum, 1992). Again, returning to the film analogy, you can benefit from thinking of your lessons as scenes in a movie. Each scene needs to be thought of in terms of the desired results or what it is we want students to be able to do by the end of the lesson (for more details, see chapter 3, page 43). Once learning goals are clear, you can begin to think of activities that will lead to the goal (Marzano & Marzano, 2001; Wiggins & McTighe, 2011).

This is where clarity becomes essential. If you think about goals with clarity, it becomes much easier to communicate expectations to students. When working with teachers in the area of increasing clarity, I ask them what tasks or activities they would like students to work on. Often, the directives lack clarity, which becomes evident when I ask teachers what it is they expect as a result of their directives. Their answer, not surprisingly, when they think of the task from the perspective of the student is "I'm not sure." Therefore, it is essential to reflect on your expectations from the vantage point of the student. Put yourself where your students are to ensure that the activity or task is clearly communicated.

An example might illuminate this point. I've observed in language classes where teachers have given students a text and asked them to write a reflection. Most students stare at their blank sheet of paper or laptop, unable to begin because the task is unclear. Rather, teachers could provide students with more specific directives in the form of questions, such as, Did the author use figurative language effectively? Why or why not? Were there enough examples stated in the passage to convince you of the author's perspective? Why or why not? In a history class, a teacher might ask students to compare two primary documents. Again, students are likely to struggle, unsure of what is being requested. Rather, increasing the clarity would require teachers to be more specific in terms of requirements, again in the form of questions, such as, Is there anything that seems unexpected in either of the primary sources? Do the images support the texts? As you read the texts, do any questions come to mind?

These and other basic strategies for supporting classroom management can be seen in the reproducible "Strategies for Improving Classroom Management" on page 86. You can use these strategies, or you can print your own blank version of this chart at **go.SolutionTree.com/instruction** to record your own ideas.

NEXT STEPS

Identify a student or students who are demonstrating misbehavior on a regular basis. For each one, determine what might be the possible cause of this misbehavior (for example, avoidance, attention seeking, or a need for stimulation). Create an action plan using strategies presented in this chapter or your own ideas. Implement it and reflect on how it went. If it wasn't successful, try another strategy. The "Template for Managing Classroom Misbehavior" (available as a reproducible on page 88) provides an exemplar and a template for this process.

Strategies for Improving Classroom Management

STRATEGY	EXAMPLES
Ensure maximum engagement of students.	During a frontal lesson, stop every few minutes for students to recode (see chapter 3, page 54, for more details) by summarizing orally with a partner or in writing. Have students create a visual of the information presented or respond to or write key questions. Also, create classroom centers or small-group activities whereby all students are engaged in a motor output such as writing, talking, calculating, or designing. As described in chapter 3 (page 43), when students are at the early stages of learning (stage 1—surface or new knowledge or stage 2—consolidation and automaticity), they should be working primarily on their own and sometimes in pairs. As they move into stage 3 (transfer), they should be working in groups.
Increase the level of student stimulation.	Direct students in need of stimulation to the back of the classroom and have them stand on one foot while they are listening to you, provide them with two desks so that they can move from one desk to the next, or allow them to go for a walk outside the classroom. However, most important, ensure that the students are actively engaged in the learning (see previous row).
Clearly articulate and reinforce rules and procedures.	Rules: Undesirable behaviors that need consequences (for example, raise your hand before speaking, speak respectfully to classmates and teachers). Procedures: Actions that require training and practice (for example, how to submit homework).
Greet students at the door.	Have a special greeting with each student. Make sure students have their materials for class.
Write a challenge on the board to engage students at the start of class.	Provide a question or prompt that can keep students occupied and focused (for example, a mathematics problem for students to solve as soon as they enter class). This task shouldn't take more than five minutes and could serve to summarize the previous lesson's goal. This will allow you a few moments to get organized, especially if you don't have your own classroom and need to move from class to class.

Page 1 of 2

Write a challenge on the board to engage students at the start of class (*continued*).	Some examples: Comment on the quote of the day, complete the mathematics example, create test questions, write a paragraph that start with the following, and so on.
Begin with clear learning goals (discussed in chapter 2, page 25).	Clarify what students should know, understand, and be able to do by the end of class.
Demonstrate withitness.	Be aware of what is going on in the classroom at all times, as though you have eyes in the back of your head. When you speak with students, make sure to face the classroom so that you can see all of the students.
Redirect when needed.	For students who are off task, gently redirect them by showing them the work they should be doing.
Establish and maintain proximity.	Make sure to circulate around the classroom. Stand next to students, especially those who tend to be off task. If you are using a slideshow, make sure to have a remote so that you don't need to stand next to your laptop. Use tablets with apps that allow you to write on the whiteboard from a distance. Most important, make sure that desks are organized such that you can circulate around the class and access all students.
Apply the rule of 4:1.	Provide four positive comments for every negative comment or redirection.
Ensure your expectations are clear.	Be sure that all students are clear as to the expectations. Review classroom expectations with students, and post them on the board. Ensure pencils and pens are down, computers are closed, and all students are listening while you establish your expectations.
Improve overall preparedness.	Think of your lesson like scenes in a movie. Try to make sure that you have the necessary materials and are properly organized for each scene. Thinking of a lesson in terms of themes is also useful in terms of overall organization of the lesson. Have all materials prepared and ready to be distributed. Have extra materials present if materials were presented in a previous class, in case students have lost or misplaced theirs. For absent students, put their name on a handout and leave it in a box at the back of the room.

Page 2 of 2

Template for Managing Classroom Misbehavior

STUDENT NAME	POSSIBLE CAUSE OF MISBEHAVIOR OR TRIGGER	ALTER THE TRIGGER	TEACH REPLACEMENT BEHAVIOR	CONSEQUENCES
Johnny	Johnny is being asked to write a narrative. Johnny has a lot of difficulty with all writing tasks.	Provide Johnny with a template with the following headings. Setting: Characters: Initiating Event: Complication: Resolution:	Johnny, when you find the work too difficult for you, I'd like you to raise your hand. I'll come over to you as soon as I can. Please let me know that the work is too challenging.	Make sure that Johnny completes the narrative. He may need to stay behind to complete it if he refuses to do it during class time.

Conducting Regular
Formative Assessment

So much of the success that students experience can be attributed to the effective practice of the one who is responsible for teaching them. Nothing is taught if nothing is learned—and assessment is our best opportunity to assess what has been understood and therefore learned (Arends, 1991; Black, Harrison, Lee, Marshall, & Wiliam, 2004; Earl, 2012).

I've yet to meet a teacher who doesn't want:

- To increase student engagement and learning
- Students who clearly understand what is expected of them
- Students to become increasingly aware of their own strengths and weaknesses
- To obtain valuable information about the quality of their instruction
- To be sure that what is being taught has been learned and mastered
- To hold students to a high standard and leave a lasting mark on them

No one would challenge the complexity of our brains. Over the years, the challenge has become to gain greater insight into how our brains process information. So much of its functioning remains elusive, and yet opening up the human brain to investigate its operations would be preposterous unless significantly warranted. According to Dylan Wiliam (2017):

> The teacher's job . . . is to engineer effective learning environments for the students. The key features of effective learning environments are that they create student engagement and allow teachers, learners, and their peers to ensure that the learning is proceeding in the intended direction. The only way we can do this is through assessment. That is why assessment is, indeed, the bridge between teaching and learning. (p. 55)

Regular and ongoing assessments identify where students are struggling so that you can address problems in a timely fashion during the learning process and not at the end of it during the summative assessment (Dixson & Worrell, 2016).

This chapter begins by examining the problematic historical notion of the brain as a black box before discussing the principle of *conducting regular formative assessment* and describing the more modern theories and research surrounding this practice. It then describes the difficulties many teachers have with implementing formative assessment and provides ways for you to overcome these challenges. Several strategies for formative assessment follow, and the chapter concludes with a plan for next steps to take over the coming months.

⚡ THE CHALLENGE

The black box notion that governed much of the field of education for so many years spoke of a system that can be viewed solely in terms of input and output, and presupposed that there's no way to find out what goes on in the mind (Black et al., 2004; Black & Wiliam, 2009; Long, 1980). The thinking seemed to be *Let's just put stuff into the brain and wait to see what comes out* in the form of a summative, end-of-unit assessment.

Within an educational context, the instruction, additional resources provided to the student, rules, and procedures are the inputs that influence student learning. These external stimuli are fed into the box (the brain), and the impact of that input or learning is measured by evaluating the output (summative evaluation). When a student failed, it was considered the student's fault since, after all, the teacher had provided inputs, and therefore, if the output was insufficient, the student didn't learn—and not much could be done about it. Historically, standard practice was to use the textbook as the curriculum. It was common for teachers to use a textbook and simply hope that the student would learn and that the implicit target goals would be met, resulting in student success. If not, it was deemed a weakness in the student (the black box) rather than a challenge to the teaching methodology (Black & Wiliam, 1998b).

Black and Wiliam cautioned against this black box notion of teaching and waiting for results because, "if there are ways in which policy makers and others can give direct help and support to the everyday classroom task of achieving better learning, then surely these ways ought to be pursued vigorously" (1998b, p. 140). In fact, they presented convincing evidence that formative assessment can indeed have a very significant impact on student achievement (Black & Wiliam, 1998b; Wiliam, 2017). They went even further, stating that "they know of no other way of raising standards for which such a strong prima facie case can be made" (Black & Wiliam, 1998b, p. 139).

The most commonly seen form of evaluation in the classroom is the hand-raising process (Black & Wiliam, 2005; Leahy, Lyon, Thompson, & Wiliam, 2005), in which the teacher poses a question, students who know the answer raise their hands, and one student is chosen to respond. This is often mistakenly done in the name of formative assessment, but it really only indicates to the teacher that one student can answer the question or prompt (Black & Wiliam, 2009; Leahy et al., 2005). And when teachers throw out a question to the class, some students become very proficient "hiders"—they look down at their shoes or try to subtly hide behind the student sitting in front of them. Rather than assessing student mastery, hand raising is a chance for those who know the answer to show off their mastery while those who don't know the answer hope and pray that they won't be chosen to respond. This is a practice that I have seen in the classrooms of the novice as well as the more experienced teacher.

🌱 THE PRINCIPLE

Two groups of researchers are integral to the development of formative assessment theories—Paul Black and Dylan Wiliam, and Reuven Feuerstein. This section will present findings from both groups' research into formative assessment, delving into what this means for your classroom. It will then present the basic steps essential to formative assessment as well as discuss the challenges to formative assessment and how you can overcome these.

Black and Wiliam's Formative Assessment Theory

Notable researchers Paul Black and Dylan Wiliam challenged the black box concept with meta-cognitive studies because in their belief, the black box theory doesn't take into account whether students are in fact learning what teachers teach (Black & Wiliam, 1998b, 2009). Regular ongoing assessments, on the other hand, identify where students are struggling so that you can address problems in a timely fashion. Black and Wiliam (1998a, 1998b, 2009) argue that formative assessment, properly employed in the classroom, will help students learn what is being taught to a substantially better degree. They support this argument with evidence from their research review (Black & Wiliam,1998a).

In a speech given at the Institute of Education at the University of London, Wiliam (2009) stated, "We use evidence of student learning to adapt teaching and learning, or instruction, to meet student needs." He continued, "If you're not using the evidence to do something that you couldn't have done without the evidence, you're not doing formative assessment."

Where did the term *assessment* come from? According to Green (1998), the word *assess* comes from the Latin verb *assidere*, which means "to sit with." Integral to this definition is the relationship between the teacher and student as they work together to improve student learning. In order to do that, teachers must slow down and take the time to ascertain if what is being taught is being learned. Rather than teaching and hoping the information sticks, the focus should turn to the strategies that you employ while in the act of teaching, which will powerfully influence the outcome. In other words, it's important for you to take responsibility for the teaching, and for students to take responsibility for their learning, because one cannot succeed without the other (Arends, 1991; Ball & Cohen, 1996; Biggs, 1996, 1999; Lauermann, 2014; Mameli, Grazia, & Molinari, 2020).

In essence, continuous assessment provides ongoing information that can positively manipulate input (how you teach) and output (how and if students are learning). To put it simply, when you employ effective, research-based strategies, students do better (Black & Wiliam, 1998a). The meta-analysis reviewed by Black and Wiliam (1998a) led them to conclude that student gains in learning triggered by formative assessment are "amongst the largest ever reported for educational interventions" (p. 61).

Much of this research addresses the importance of the interactive nature of teaching and learning. If you're a teacher who asks yourself, "What can I do to increase student learning? How can I do better?" then you know that truly effective teachers monitor student learning on an ongoing basis and use the information to improve their instruction. Not only do you know this, but it's my guess that you already embrace this practice. I have yet to meet a teacher who doesn't want to strengthen his or her educational efforts, and using feedback from student work is an excellent way to help both teacher and student in this effort. Both the teacher and the student reap maximum benefit, each within their respective roles, through interaction that uses formative evaluation as its basis (Black & Wiliam, 2005, 2009; Hattie & Timperley, 2007; Nicol & Macfarlane-Dick, 2006).

You and your students make use of the formative assessment data to make adjustments: students use the data to close the gap between where they are currently and where they need to be, and you use the data to improve your instruction. According to many researchers, assessment impacts student learning more than any other single factor (Entwistle & Entwistle, 1992; Hodgson & Pang, 2012; Segers & Dochy, 2006; Struyven, Dochy, & Janssens, 2005).

Formative assessments are the heartbeat of the teaching and learning process—probably one of the most important activities you can do as a teacher—and if you're not assessing, the question becomes, How can you know for sure that you are fulfilling your purpose to effectively prepare students to move on from you? Holding standards and objectives in one hand and formative assessments in the other, tossing them back and forth to check in on how students are mastering the learning targets, can you be sure of their outcomes, or are you guessing? According to Tomlinson and McTighe (2006), "Assessment focuses on gathering information about student achievement to make instructional decisions. Grading is an end-point judgment about student achievement" (p. 71). Formative assessment keeps those of us responsible for educating students up to date with what they understand and informs us that we don't have to wait for output (Black & Wiliam, 2009; Earl, 2012).

Black and Wiliam (1998a) focused specifically on the role of grades versus comments and their effect on student performance. What they found was that grades alone and grades with comments both had a very limited impact on student growth (Black & Wiliam, 1998a). Even when we write comments, when grades are present, students focus solely on their mark—thinking either "I did well" or "I didn't do well"—and the comments become superfluous. The most significant student growth occurs when we provide students with comments pertaining to their work in a timely fashion about ways in which it can be improved.

The second theory crucial to a discussion on formative assessment belongs to Dr. Reuven Feuerstein.

Feuerstein's Theory of Cognitive Modifiability

Feuerstein, a psychologist who studied under Piaget at the University of Geneva, developed the theory of cognitive modifiability because he believed that when we modify the learning environment of students with special needs, we increase their ability to make sense of the world around them (Feuerstein et al., 1981; Feuerstein, Rand, Hoffman, Hoffman, & Miller, 1979). He developed a series of assessment and learning tools, referred to as *instrumental enrichment* (IE), that were aimed at enhancing students' cognitive functions necessary for academic learning and achievement.

The fundamental assumption of IE is that intelligence is *not* static or fixed, like the black box we discussed earlier in this chapter; rather, intelligence is dynamic and modifiable (Feuerstein et al., 1979). These tools seek to modify the fundamental thinking skills, to provide students with all that is necessary and available to function as independent learners, increase their motivation, and develop metacognition—in short, to "learn how to learn."

Feuerstein used a series of fourteen instruments that are content-free and aimed at teaching the child how to think. Examples of these tools are organization of dots, orientation in space, comparisons, and categorization (International Renewal Institute, n.d.). The teacher takes on the role of mediator, guiding the student to think, reflect, and engage in effective metacognitive approaches to learning.

Feuerstein called the process of adult guidance supporting children to modify cognitive potential *mediation*. This method looks at each student's strengths as well as weaknesses to understand how the student learns (Feuerstein, Feuerstein, & Falik, 2015; Feuerstein & Jensen, 1980). Slowly, incrementally, the student's cognition begins to change, and tasks and concepts he or she could not understand before start to make sense. By the end of a year of intervention, the incremental changes add up to meaningful, lasting improvements.

Inherent in Feuerstein's model is the vital role of the educator in the child's life. Much like Vygotsky (1978) and his model of the ZPD, Feuerstein believed that the educator has vital influence in altering the way in which the child responds to stimuli in his surroundings (Feuerstein, Klein, & Tannenbaum, 1991). To illustrate, imagine the student is faced with a stimulus—perhaps a staircase or a mathematics problem—and the student is expected to respond to the stimulus with some output. The mediator, as termed by Feuerstein (Feuerstein et al., 2015; Feuerstein & Jensen, 1980), using a guided approach, enables the student to make sense of the stimulus and understand how to engage or respond. The response becomes increasingly more sophisticated as a result of scaffolding provided by the mediator.

Obviously you have limited control over many of the risk factors with which students come into the classroom—and yet, there's so much you can do to provide students with preventative factors that can shield them from the impact of the risk factors. Returning to the notion of the classroom as an ecosystem, within this system, each student is valued for his or her contribution to the overall environment. The belief in every student's capacity and imparting to all students the value that they bring to the environment is a powerful preventative factor.

This, however, cannot be properly employed without the ongoing collection of data to support the approach. To effectively employ Feuerstein's IE, it is important to have the following mindset and understanding.

- Cognition is modifiable.

- Assessments should fit into your teaching routine.

- Whenever possible, use the data you collect to work with students so that they build their abilities into lasting improvements.

This interdependent relationship between the mediator and the learner relies on effective formative assessment. This will be discussed in the following section.

The Basic Steps Essential to Formative Assessment

According to Hattie (2008), in his examination of over eight hundred studies, ongoing assessment has a significant effect on student achievement. With this ongoing loop of teaching and assessing, the teacher becomes a student of his or her own teaching (Hattie, 2008), because the assessments are used to evaluate not only if students are mastering the goals but also if teachers are teaching effectively.

So now that we know what formative assessment is—a collection of data from the students to see if they are mastering skills and content (Black & Wiliam, 2009)—how can teachers employ it and use the subsequent data to support student learning and identify small gaps in acquisition before these small gaps become much larger and more difficult to remediate? According to Wiggins and McTighe (1998) and Heritage (2011), assessment must include certain factors in order for it to effectively chart a course for students, informing them as to what is going well and what needs further investment, both from them and from the teacher.

As articulated so well by Black and Wiliam (2012):

> The teacher is responsible for designing and implementing an effective learning environment, and the learner is responsible for the learning within that environment. Furthermore, since the responsibility for learning rests with both the teacher and the learner, it is incumbent on each to do all they can to mitigate the impact of any failures of the other. (p. 208)

As such, the relationship between teachers and students is symbiotic: neither can do their jobs or maintain their roles in the process without the other. For this relationship to function effectively, it's important that the teacher establishes an environment conducive to thriving. When you organize your responsibilities, the student will have access to readily available support: academic, technological, emotional, and social. Within the environment of the classroom that you create, students then need to do their part: they need to take responsibility for taking their seats on time, doing their work, and participating in group or class discussions. This prepares the classroom for the exchange of information between the teacher and students in the instruction process and is critical to the effectiveness of the classroom environment (Giallo & Little, 2003; Martella et al., 2003; Marzano & Marzano, 2001).

The first step essential to formative assessment is the formulation and clear articulation of learning goals, highlighted in chapter 2 (page 25; Cleary et al., 2017; Marzano & Brown, 2009; McTighe & Wiggins, 1999; Whetten, 2007; Wiggins & McTighe, 1998, 2011). It's important for you to be a big-picture thinker, setting the learning goals, executing effective teaching practices, and providing indicators of mastery along the way. For example, if students need to know how to add fractions with unlike denominators, the formative assessment will need to assess if they can in fact do this. If the learning goal indicates that students need to know the elements of an effective persuasive text, the evaluation will need to assess if students can list the elements of a persuasive text. Important here is to evaluate the listed target goals as opposed to goals that are not listed. In the example regarding persuasive text, the goal addresses the need not to know how to write a text, but only to know the elements. Therefore, the assessment needs to ascertain if students know the elements. Granted, linking goals to assessment can be tricky, but it's essential. The teaching requires deliberate interventions to provide meaningful exchanges and to ensure knowing when mastery occurs and at what level.

The second step is to explain to your students these learning goals, and in particular what they should be able to do by the end of the lesson (Biggs, 1996, 1999; McTighe & Wiggins, 1999; Tomlinson & McTighe, 2006; Wiggins & McTighe, 1998, 2011). If, for example, your goal is for students to understand a concept, what does that really mean? Do you want your students to be able to recall facts? Summarize or apply information? Predict something? Analyze or compare something? Evaluate arguments? A combination of these? Do the assessments measure whether students have met the learning goals? Be specific in identifying the goals of the lesson or unit, and if the formative assessment is meaningful and has value, it will likely be so only if and when you have clearly established and communicated the target goals.

The third step is to develop and assign an assessment instrument (Shepard, 2000). The assessment could be a quick pencil-and-paper test, or the ability to use rich vocabulary in a second-language class when conversing with a partner. Explain to your students what you want them to do and to get from the exercise.

There are many examples of ongoing assessments that can be used, but most important is to develop an expansive repertoire of ideas and to decide among the many ideas that are most conducive to student growth. For example, you might have just presented a critical concept (perhaps Gallicanism) in a high school history class. Given the essential nature of the concept, you could take a minute to ask all students (ongoing formative assessment is only effective when all students engage in it) to write down the definition of that term before moving on. With a quick circulation, you'll have visible evidence as to whether the students can accurately define this term. Nearing the end of a unit, the formative assessments are likely to be more complex as they will require students to integrate concepts and skills. Technology can be extremely useful. There are many digital tools that can be accessed to elicit quick responses from students, such as Flipgrid, Kahoot, Plickers, and Socrative. Edutopia (www.edutopia.org/article /7-smart-fast-ways-do-formative-assessment) is another useful website with formative assessment ideas.

The fourth step is to evaluate performance and provide feedback on the assessment you assigned (Black & Wiliam, 2005, 2009; Hattie & Timperley, 2007; Nicol & Macfarlane-Dick, 2006). Feedback based on the evidence—student work—must indicate what needs to be improved on. If a teacher writes the comment "too vague" on a student's assignment, the student won't know what he or she needs to do to improve—the comment itself is too vague and offers no guidance the student can learn from. If a teacher provides feedback stating that the mathematics calculation is incorrect, it also needs to identify the problem that led to the error: Were the steps followed? Was the wrong formula applied? Ultimately, the feedback must inform and guide rather than merely state what is wrong (Saphier & Gower, 1997).

THE IMPORTANCE OF EVIDENCE

I once asked a teacher who was working on reading skills with a struggling learner how the student was doing. The teacher told me that she was doing great! I then asked him how he knew and what he saw that indicated to him that she was doing so well. He responded with, "She never wanted to come out of class for help, but now she runs out whenever she

continued →

sees me." The problem with this comment is that it isn't an indicator of learning-goal mastery. After determining the acceptable evidence of mastery, the next step is to decide by what criteria you will judge mastery. This distinction is often difficult to grasp, because once you have determined what mastery will look like, you think you're done. Jonathan Saphier and Robert Gower (1997) argue in *The Skillful Teacher* that "the clearest articulation of the objective appears in the assessment task and its criteria for success" (p. 509).

The fifth, and final, step is to reflect on overall mastery of the learning goals and development of strategies to help students gain more success (Hattie, 2012; Hockett & Doubet, 2013; McTighe & O'Connor, 2009). The collection of data provides you with an understanding of student needs and where you need to adjust lesson plan designs to ensure that students continuously improve. The data collected are also useful in determining the effectiveness of instruction. It's necessary to reserve time for the students who require feedback for an incorrect response or misconception (for example, dividing fractions by multiplying the denominator, which can lead to continued misinformation). Information gleaned from this process can—and should—be used to identify learning gaps before they show up in a summative assessment. Provide feedback and do something about it in a timely fashion. Most of the time, you'll find that it will be a quick loopback with only a few students needing immediate attention. Rather than review a concept or skill with the entire class when only a handful need the review, those students who don't need the review can be engaged in an anchor activity (for more information, see chapter 6, page 109).

Ultimately, formative assessment is a win-win-win. First, those who need the review get it without lagging behind; second, those who have mastered the skill or concept are engaged in an activity that is relevant and challenging, sharpening their skills; and third, teachers are actively ensuring that what they taught has been learned. The steps to implementing formative assessment are summarized in table 5.1.

Table 5.1: Steps to Implementing Formative Assessment

STEPS	EXAMPLES
Step 1: Clearly formulate and articulate learning goals.	*Students will know*: the definition of literary devices (simile, metaphor, personification). *Students will know:* how to identify a literary device in a piece of text. *Students will understand that:* authors use literary devices to persuade, entertain, inform, and connect to the reader. By the end of class students will be able to: *define* the following literary devices (*simile, hyperbole, personification*) and *identify* the literary device in the passage and identify what they think the author's purpose was in using the particular device.
Step 2: Explain to your students these learning goals and, in particular, what they should be able to do by the end of the lesson.	"Students, in today's class we're going to be learning about literary devices. By the end of class my goal is for you to know . . . and to understand that . . . By the end of class you should be able to do the following . . ."

Step 3: Develop and assign an assessment instrument.	An assessment tool could look like this.
	
	    Define the following literary devices.
	
	    • Simile:
	
	    • Personification:
	
	    • Hyperbole:
	
	    Please highlight each of these literary tools in the following text.

Step 4: Evaluate performance and provide feedback on the assessment that was assigned.	Quickly review each student's work. Pay attention especially to those who incorrectly defined the terms.
Step 5: Reflect on overall mastery of the learning goals and develop strategies to help students gain more success.	At the start of the following class, you could provide students with a writing prompt and ask those students who mastered the goals from the previous day to write a short text using simile, personification, and hyperbole while you review the concepts with those students who didn't show mastery of the terms.

Ultimately, feedback is used to improve teaching, which will improve student learning (Black & Wiliam, 2005, 2009; Hattie, 2008; Hattie & Timperley, 2007). When teachers prepare well-established and clearly articulated learning goals followed by formative assessments, they create a dynamic atmosphere where both the teacher and the student thrive.

The Perceived Difficulty of Formative Assessment

Given the importance of formative assessment and your commitment to student success, why does it remain such an elusive practice for so many educators? (Heritage, 2007; Shepard, 2000; Volante & Beckett, 2011). The two most common answers are "It takes too much time" and "I wanted to do it, but couldn't because it wasn't built into my teaching plan."

Formative Assessment Takes Too Much Time

One concern is that utilizing formative assessment takes too much time away from teaching, but assessments do not have to consume significant amounts of class time to be constructive (Marzano et al., 2003; Nadelson et al., 2016). The data collection can be quick and easy to digest. At times, a quick "define the term" assessment that students write in class can serve to inform you on student progress. You can circulate to rapidly verify if students have accurately defined the term. Digital tools are very useful for avoiding paper and getting instantaneous results about whether students choose the correct term or provide the correct response to a prompt. These tools are especially useful at the high school level, where teachers see many students each day.

Even with these quick checks, it is clear that formative assessment does consume some time. However, in the long run, it actually saves you time because you won't be faced with untangling information, content, or skills that either have not been mastered initially or have been misunderstood, leading to further misunderstandings (Hattie, 2012; Hockett & Doubet, 2013; McTighe & O'Connor, 2009). Without gathering information about what students learn, education goes back to the era of the black box, in which teachers hoped and prayed that learning was taking place but did not know if it really was. Educators can't afford to let that happen.

The idea with frequent, ongoing assessments is that it is often sufficient to simply peruse the responses to determine who has and who hasn't mastered the goal. Data need to be collected often; otherwise you'll need to provide lengthy responses to all students, all the time—and of course, in this situation, you will become easily frustrated or impatient. As unusual as it sounds, teachers do not need to provide feedback constantly to students who consistently respond accurately when the prompt, question, or task is fact-based and binary (either you know it or you don't). Therefore, keep in mind that formative assessments are meant to be a quick way to ascertain if students are heading toward the intended goal. Most often these are quick check-ins not intended to take more than a few minutes for students to write and for you to review. Near the start of a new unit of study, these check-ins are intentionally short. As the unit of study progresses and students become more knowledgeable, the assessments could take the form of short quizzes.

Formative Assessment Wasn't Part of the Teaching Plan

Time management also seems to be a barrier preventing effective formative assessment. You might have every intention of collecting data about student learning, but suddenly the bell rings, and there goes the data collection. No matter how long or short the lesson, formative assessment should always be a natural part of the lesson (Black & Wiliam, 2009; Nicol & Macfarlane-Dick, 2006; Wiliam, 2014). To ensure that evaluation becomes a part of all lessons, it's best for you to allot time within each class for assessment.

Teachers can trust the results from these assessments because they relate directly to instructional standards set forth by the teacher in his or her lesson goals. Additionally, results are immediate and relevant to the individual student. In essence, assessments are not separate from the teaching and learning process; they are an intrinsic part of it (Black & Wiliam, 1998a, 1998b, 2005; Wiliam, 2009, 2014). When they become an integral part of the instructional process as a means to help students learn, this becomes a time-saving teaching tactic with tremendous benefits that are boundless for both teachers and students.

🌐 THE STRATEGY

This section discusses in depth two strategies you can use for formative assessment.

1. Reciprocal teaching
2. Response cards

Additional formative assessment strategies can be found in the reproducible "Formative Assessment Strategies" on page 106.

Reciprocal Teaching

Early on in my career, I worked with a large group of high school students who had great difficulty with comprehension. I worked with this group each day using *reciprocal teaching* (RT), a comprehension strategy developed by Brown and Palincsar (1987) and studied by other researchers (Mulyono, Asmawi, & Nuriah, 2018; Pilten, 2016). After I taught some content or a new concept, I would ask the students to develop questions that could test their understanding, much like the questions that they would find on a teacher-made comprehension test. Using the "I do, we do, you do one, you do many" strategy, I guided students in how to ask good questions to test their comprehension. At first, their questions were far too basic and detail oriented, such as "What color was the main character's hair?" This showed that they had not understood the key ideas of the paragraph. Many of the students also failed to stop and identify a phrase that they read but didn't understand. Similar to many poor comprehenders, they would continue reading without pause. When I sensed that they hadn't understood the passage, or had misread a word in the passage, I would stop them and ask them a question about what they had just read, or what a word meant. In fact, it turned out they did not understand what they had read, but rather than stop and reread the passage, they continued reading—presumably because they had grown accustomed to not understanding what they were reading. It was through this constant and ongoing formative evaluation that I was able to guide them effectively. I was learning along with my students and beginning to understand my role as the mediator, seeking feedback so that I could effectively guide my instruction, enabling my students to become strategic learners. I modeled how to ask good questions, how to effectively summarize a passage, how to predict what was coming next in a text, or the importance of stopping and rereading a passage when it is unclear to you. I would stop periodically to assess their use of the strategies and their overall understanding of the passage. It was through this feedback provided by students that I was able to guide them to a more sophisticated and consistent use of the strategies.

Receiving this feedback was imperative because it guided me in terms of what seemed to be working and what remained difficult, so that I could adjust my teaching methods. I can recall almost to the day when the students "got it." Their questions were focused on key information, and they stopped when a phrase was not understood. One student actually said, "Wait a second—I don't understand this word." This moment was truly one to celebrate. They were becoming sophisticated comprehenders who were engaging with the text they were reading.

When students roll their eyes each time you review strategies or a procedure involved in developing a skill, I invite you to consider this a great sign that these strategies are becoming integrated into the students' repertoire. As described in chapter 3 (page 43), scaffolding forms the foundation here as you gradually relinquish control and the students develop expertise with the implementation of the strategies (Hogan & Pressley, 1997; Pea, 2004; van de Pol et al., 2010; Vygotsky, 1978). Please consider doing as I have learned to do: each day, review the strategies, model their use, and engage in a process of guided practice with the students. You will recognize poor comprehenders growing into sophisticated comprehenders right before your very eyes.

In 1933, John Dewey, one of the world's most influential psychologists, philosophers, and educators and known for his philosophy of pragmatism, highlighted the value of reflecting on one's experiences. It is not the experience itself that helps individuals learn, but rather their reflections on these experiences that are critical to their learning (Dewey, 1993). In other words, it is not the act of engagement alone that creates learning and forms new memories; rather, it is the opportunity teachers afford to students to reflect on their learning (Evertson, 1994; Marzano, Pickering, & Pollock, 2001). This can only occur if students have the time and the opportunity to offer their feedback to the teacher regarding what they have learned or haven't learned—which occurs when they are assessed. Students are becoming purposeful learners, just as you are honing your ability to be purposeful in your teaching.

Response Cards

According to Margaret Heritage (2011), "The essential purpose of formative assessment as a practice is to move the student learning forward while their learning is still in the process of developing." Ongoing assessment is the guidepost for the teacher to ensure that the students are in fact learning what the teacher has taught (Heritage, 2007, 2010). It is intended to answer two very important questions: (1) How well are students learning? and (2) How effectively are teachers teaching? (Angelo & Patricia-Cross, 1993). It therefore becomes the visible evidence that the learning goals are or are not being mastered. It is the D in KUD. Teachers begin by identifying the K (what students need to know), then the U (what the main concept is and why it's important), and finally the D—evidence that the student has learned.

- If the K is *know* the definition of these terms, the D or *formative evaluation* is to define the terms.

- If the K is *how* to find the perimeter of a shape, the D or *formative assessment* is to calculate the perimeter of a shape.

- If the K is *how* to write an introduction or topic sentence, the D or *formative assessment* is to write a topic sentence.

Response cards are a great and quick strategy for assessing the D of KUD through formative assessment. In this strategy, students use cards to quickly indicate to the teacher a response, question, or feeling about the lesson. The teacher is then able to assess learning across the entire group in a very short period of time. For example, the teacher shows a prompt (such as the number 3), and students have to hold up a card indicating if it's a prime or composite number. The teacher can scan for incorrect responses and decide whether to keep teaching about prime and composite numbers or to move on.

Or, students could write down the muddiest point—the most confusing idea—and the teacher could identify which areas of the subject need elaboration or additional review. Alternatively, students could use response cards to summarize the main ideas of a lesson for a student who is absent, allowing the teacher to see what ideas have been transferred to most students and which ones might still need work. These are not the summative or end-of-unit evaluations; rather, they are ongoing daily checks to indicate to the teacher how students are doing on their way toward the larger end or summative unit goals.

THE VALUE OF FORMATIVE ASSESSMENT FOR THE TEACHER, NOT ONLY THE STUDENT

Many years ago, I walked into a second-grade class to help out a teacher who was new to the practice of formative assessment. He had just completed a story and wanted to evaluate student retention of some of the key aspects. He wrote down four questions on the board and asked students to respond to each one, individually, on a sheet of paper. The students seemed a bit anxious about having their knowledge tested, so to calm them down, I asked the students, "Who, in fact, is being tested?" They paused for a moment, thought about the question, and then a few students shouted, "The teacher is!"

The assessments that students complete each lesson are the teacher's best sign as to whether or not the learning was effective (Black & Wiliam, 2005, 2009; Wiliam, 2014). In this sense, both teacher and students are learners. Students are learning new knowledge, concepts, and skills, and teachers are learning how to increase the effectiveness of their instruction and overall engagement with students.

A statement by John Hattie about the influence that teacher evaluations have on student achievement has proven itself time and time again to be fundamentally true. According to Hattie (2012),

> The interactions between what we do as educators and what students are doing as learners is key: it is the interactions—and being tuned into the nature and impact of these interactions—that is critical. (p. 160)

When the teachers I work with evaluate the effectiveness of their own teaching practices on student learning, they make more calculated interventions and provide students with multiple opportunities and alternatives to learn, at both surface and deep levels. Once you start replacing "I talk, I teach, they learn" with "Are my students mastering what I teach?" you're putting yourself in the mind frame in which you see your role in evaluating your effectiveness as an educator.

The reproducible "Formative Assessment Strategies" (page 106) contains some strategies discussed in this chapter along with others. You can choose to implement these strategies, or print a blank version of the reproducible and write your own in the blank rows.

NEXT STEPS

Begin your next class with a clear articulation of the learning goals: what students will need to know, understand, and be able to do by the end of class. Identify what you will ask them to do (the D in KUD) by the end of class in the reproducible "Formative Assessment Ideas" on page 108. Make sure to communicate to them what they will need to do by the end of class to show mastery. Try some of the assessments in the reproducible "Formative Assessment Strategies" on page 106, or create your own quick formative check of the material.

Formative Assessment Strategies

STRATEGY	EXAMPLE
Completing the problem	Students who were just taught a math procedure such as adding fractions with like denominators would be given an example to complete.
Writing a sample	Have students write a paragraph to show evidence that they learned how to write a topic sentence, a complete sentence, or any other writing skill taught during the lesson.
Defining terms	Have students define a list of vocabulary terms—for example: Define each of these terms related to digestion. • Mouth • Pharynx • Epiglottis • Esophagus
Paraphrasing to summarize	Teach students to use the following summarizing language. • So what I'm hearing is . . . • The bottom line then seems to be . . . • Let me make sure I have this right . . . You're saying that . . . Or • So what the author is saying is . . . • In other words . . . • The gist of it is . . .

3-2-1	Have students write down:
	- Three new concepts or ideas that they learned
	- Two questions that they still have
	- One way that they can now apply the concept
Response cards	Ask students a question such as "What is the definition of a prime number?" Then have all students write the answer on their whiteboards or response cards.
A note to an absent student	Ask students to explain the essential concepts, review the steps, or summarize facts for a student who is not in school today.
I used to think but now I know	After a concept has been explained (for example, stereotyping), ask students to write down what they thought it meant prior to instruction, and what they now know it means.

Formative Assessment Ideas

LEARNING GOALS (KUD) By the end of the lesson I want my students to know, understand, and be able to do the following.	FORMATIVE ASSESSMENT IDEAS (Remember, these must be identical or at least in line with the D.)	REFLECTIONS
K: U: D:		
K: U: D:		
K: U: D:		
K: U: D:		
K: U: D:		
K: U: D:		

Employing Differentiated Instruction for All Students

The answer to the question, Do teachers matter? is absolutely, positively yes—teachers matter greatly in the formation and education of their students. As educators, you indeed make a difference in the lives of your students, and the difference you make will either positively or negatively impact the student's future (Polick, Cullen, & Buskist, 2010). It's important that you know this and believe it to be true so you can show up for your students with a deep knowledge and understanding not only of your course material but also of the students as individuals. Knowing students, their needs, and their unique traits as well as ways in which their learning needs can be met within the context of the classroom is the essence of differentiated instruction.

In 2003, John Hattie, under the auspices of the Australian Council for Educational Research, examined the role of teachers in the overall success of student learning. In *Teachers Make a Difference, What Is the Research Evidence?* Hattie (2003) discusses the research evidence showing that "it is what teachers know, do, and care about that is very powerful in the learning equation" (p. 2). Despite a number of factors related to student success, the only two that have any meaningful impact are (1) factors inherent in the student, such as prior knowledge and overall competence, and (2) teacher efficacy (Hattie, 2003). Further, and most critical to the question, Do teachers matter? is this finding: given the limited influence that teachers have over factors inherent in the student, the factor that accounts for the greatest level of variance and impact is the teacher (Hattie, 2003; Stronge & Tucker, 2000). In order for students to succeed, it's of critical importance that we all believe in their success (Hattie, 2003; Polick et al., 2010).

To further understand the factors that influence students' academic success, Hattie (2008) conducted meta-analyses to identify the factors leading toward or detracting from student academic achievement. Whereas most of the strategies he identified in 2003 and then again in 2016 had positive effects, he did find some exceptionally effective strategies. According to the vast number of studies he reviewed, most of the top strategies, such as providing students with feedback, checking for understanding, communicating learning goals, and giving direct instruction, directly relate to teacher effectiveness (Killian, 2014). Because of the very significant impact that you have in the lives of your students, differentiation that is perceived as a value and not merely as a practice is essential.

For those not familiar with its history, differentiated instruction was officially introduced to the education community in 1999 with Carol Ann Tomlinson's book *The Differentiated Classroom: Responding to the Needs of All Learners.* Defined as adapting content, process, or product according to a specific student's readiness, interest, and learning profile (Hall, 2002; Tomlinson, 1999), differentiated instruction was a seminal addition to the field because it presented educators with a model that could be used to meet the overwhelming challenge of addressing diverse academic, behavioral, and social needs in the classroom (Tomlinson, 1999).

The goal of a differentiated classroom is maximum student growth and individual success (Tomlinson, 1999). As schools now exist, the goal is often to bring all students to grade level or to ensure that each student masters a prescribed set of skills in a specified length of time. Teachers then measure students' progress only against a predetermined standard. Such a goal is appropriate, and understanding where a child's learning is relative to a benchmark is important. However, when an entire class moves forward to study new skills and concepts without any individual adjustments in time or support, some students are doomed to fail (Kosanovich, Weinstein, & Goldman, 2009; Tomlinson, 1999, 2001). Similarly, classrooms typically contain other students who can demonstrate mastery of grade-level skills and material to be understood before the school year begins—or who could do so in a fraction of the time teachers would spend "teaching" them (Tomlinson, 1999, 2001). These learners often receive an A, but that mark is more an acknowledgment of their advanced starting point relative to grade-level expectations than a reflection of serious growth. In a differentiated classroom, you could use grade-level benchmarks as one tool for charting a child's learning path. However, you could also carefully chart individual growth. You could also measure personal success, at least in part, on individual growth from the learner's starting point (Tomlinson, 2001)—whatever that might be. Given all of the research on the importance of effort, the journey traveled from the student's starting point to his or her current level of performance is more indicative of future success than is the summative grade (Perkins & Blythe, 1994).

For effective differentiated instruction to take place, school leaders must encourage and support differentiated instruction in the classroom—but how can this be done when differentiation is rooted in ineffective classroom practice? As you've likely already experienced for yourself, this doesn't help the student; it only serves to further frustrate you. Student learning is most effective in classrooms that offer a positive, challenging, and supportive learning environment and—I cannot stress this enough—one in which persistent formative assessments are applied to ensure that you and your students know what steps are most likely to propel them forward. Formative assessments are truly necessary to effectively apply differentiated instruction. Additionally, when you wholeheartedly believe in something that you propose, it'll be easier to convince the students in your classroom that it's worth the hard work required from them.

This chapter begins by explaining the challenges associated with applying differentiation to only a subset of the students in the class, rather than the whole class. Next, it will describe the principle of *employing differentiated instruction for all students* and address the importance of believing in differentiation for all. It will also discuss the implications regarding fairness that often surround discussions of differentiated instruction. It then describes several strategies you can use as you begin applying this principle in your classroom, and concludes with a plan for next steps to take over the coming months.

⚡ THE CHALLENGE

The demands on teachers to meet the individual needs of their students are formidable. Many of the models presented decades ago are still being applied in schools today in spite of how the world, times, and people have changed over these many decades. Therefore, the challenge to adapt instruction to the needs of the learner is something that has not quite been resolved.

In 1953, *Educational Leadership* devoted an entire issue to the challenges in meeting individual needs (Snyder, 1953). Since the early 1900s, many models were put in place to address the phenomenon of diversity in the classroom such as mastery learning, individualized instruction, ability grouping, and universal promotions of all students (Washburne, 1953). In the same issue, an article was written on the unique needs of adolescents and the importance of providing them with authentic and meaningful learning experiences in an environment of discovery (Brundage, 1953). If these ideas and models have been around for so long, how can we be more able to understand their application and apply them on a more consistent basis in our schools today? We must take advantage of the tools and strategies that over the past decades have shown that it is possible to ease the teaching process within diverse classrooms.

✿ THE PRINCIPLE

If you believe that all students can succeed, and that their success is closely tied to both your belief in their success and your belief that your teaching practices will influence their success, you're far more likely to engage in differentiation. In this regard, differentiation is first and foremost a value or a belief rather than a model to be applied when student needs demand it. Differentiation must transition from a model that focuses primarily on the diverse needs of students to a value or call to action for teachers and for all students.

It's important not to be misled by the concept of differentiation as a tactic, or something to be done sometimes and only for some students. For example, this misunderstanding of differentiation is reflected in the following quote heard from a high school teacher:

> As long as I am required to identify my students' unique, idiosyncratic needs and respond accordingly, I can connect the dots and assume that if I don't perceive there to be outliers in this classroom, strategies or tactics for differentiation are not required, or the needs are too significant and therefore this model is ineffective.

I've heard many times, "Differentiation can work in some classrooms but not all"; however, if we shift the conversation from differentiation being merely a series of tactics to the belief that *all* students have needs you must meet with certain strategies, and that you as the teacher are at the core of student success, the application of effective learning principles will result in success for students. At times, you may need to dig deeper in your toolbox of effective strategies to respond to the needs of those with more significant challenges, but if your belief system calls on you to meet everyone's needs, it is simply a given that you will need to dig. When differentiation is for all, it becomes impervious to classroom makeup or individual student profiles because it is part of who you are as an educator (Tomlinson, 1999). We need to start thinking of differentiation as a value that is supported by a series of tactics that you learn and implement to operationalize the value, rather than merely a series of strategies to be applied when the need arises.

Tomlinson (2003) explains it best when she states that "while students share the same basic needs, these needs will manifest themselves in different ways depending on the student's gender, culture, general life experiences, talents, interests, learning preferences, affective development, cognitive development, and support systems" (p. 19). It's what you do next that matters. So, as we search for the Holy Grail in student success, it's your responsibility to look at yourself and decide what you can and must do to create classroom environments where all students are comfortable being themselves within their learning environment so they don't just *have* to be there; they *want* to be there.

When You Believe, They Believe

Finally, after decades and decades of struggles in the pursuit of addressing diversity in the classroom, there is a model—differentiated instruction—to address this often insurmountable challenge, and yet, with all great hope and many hours in teacher training sessions, it has not been easy for some teachers to transfer the theory to practice. Some teachers would exhibit microelements of differentiation strategies, almost like a magician showing the audience a newly mastered trick. They could be heard saying, "I think I need to differentiate today," or "This is a strong class, so there is no need to differentiate." This approach to differentiation is at odds with meaningful change, and will naturally leave teachers feeling underwhelmed with long-term results. With this way of thinking, teachers will give up trying and gradually return to their usual teaching styles and patterns.

Here's the thing: any theory that will ultimately lead to meaningful change for students has to become part of the heart and soul of the classroom rather than a visitor that appears infrequently. The translation of this theory into practice requires that it become a core value, an essential part of the teaching framework, and not "another thing to do."

Facilitating teacher growth in differentiation is more about knowing what matters and realizing that learning happens *in* us more so than *to* us. Providing leadership to teachers with the skills to teach differently fosters continual growth in them and helps them throughout their careers in the classroom to help *all* students become better learners (Heacox, 2012; Tomlinson, 2014).

It is important to remember that when you believe all students can succeed, the students will believe it. Not a school year goes by that I don't hear teachers tell me that certain weak students won't pass an exam or a course because they don't have the prerequisite skills, or that specific students aren't applying themselves or aren't motivated enough to succeed. And yet, when the same teachers shift their thinking away from "This student is this or that; therefore I can't help," to "All students need to succeed, and success is different for everyone . . . so now what strategies can I use?" and they increase effectiveness by employing differentiated strategies, the classroom dynamic changes, and the student more than likely responds (Bucholz & Sheffler, 2009; Grubaugh & Houston, 1990; Tomlinson, 2014). The beliefs and expectations you have about your students' capabilities directly affect their performance and achievements. When you believe individual students can achieve a learning goal and provide them with opportunities to succeed, they take into effect your belief in them and accept your beliefs as part of who they are. Therefore, beyond having and using a tool kit of strategies, it's imperative to take into consideration the subtle but powerful effect that your beliefs and expectations have on your students.

One of the great privileges in my educational career is that of watching the beauty of this unfold between educators and their students, and when it becomes the stubborn and relentless nature of educators to believe that every student can succeed, the students apply themselves and do. Believe in all students, but also know that success means different things to every student. We already know that not every student will become a mathematics expert, historian, or prolific writer, but all weak students can do better today than they did yesterday—especially when they can see and feel that their educators believe in them.

Differentiation Is Not a To-Do List Item

In spite of having to confront fundamental issues of diversity within our classrooms, if we say we want to create learning environments in schools where all learners are seen as capable of achieving desired outcomes, then we have to begin with the belief that they are. Thus, rather than simply being another thing to do, differentiation becomes a core value maintained by you, and a wonderful opportunity to profoundly impact students' belief in themselves. If you don't believe in both your students *and* your ability to impact their trajectory in life, it won't happen. Students are profoundly influenced by the messages you send regarding their ability. When you build belief as a core value in yourself, you inspire your students to believe in themselves. What a gift!

Therefore, before we place demands on our teachers to differentiate the material to meet the needs of all their students, it's critical for teachers to accept that differentiation is not "oh no, another task to do," but rather a core value that they maintain when speaking to students, treating each one as a unique individual with his or her own unique needs.

It is important to note that the support that teachers provide to students must be viewed in holistic terms rather than as a day-to-day checklist. While educators should aspire to meet all students' needs each day, it's not likely to occur. Not all students' academic, behavioral, and social needs will be addressed all the time, but when teachers are cognizant of whose needs were not addressed today, they can try to meet them tomorrow. If there are too many needs for you to address each day, identify those that are most urgent. In addition, reaching out to colleagues for support can be very effective. They may have differentiated strategies in their toolbox that you can try in your class.

Differentiation and the Concept of Fairness

The notion of what is *fair* poses a challenge for many teachers struggling to implement differentiation. Providing students with different options based on interest levels seems to be an acceptable method of differentiating, but once teachers move into the arena of differentiating by content or readiness levels, the sentiment many hold is that such differentiation isn't fair to those who are required to master the learning goals without any modifications.

In many jurisdictions, teachers cannot make modifications to the final unit goals, and assessments must be standardized for all students. Despite this, there are many opportunities to address individual readiness levels within a unit plan, even if at the end of the unit the teacher must hold all students to the same standards.

Unfortunately, you're not able to will students to reach lesson and unit goals. The only way to ensure they do is by providing them with additional time, quality instruction needed to master the content knowledge and skills, and activities that enable them to practice the requisite skills before moving on (Guskey, 2010; Marzano, 2009b; Rosenshine, 2009). The teacher simply must address the needs of such students (McTighe & Brown, 2005). This is most obvious in courses such as mathematics, where skills are cumulative. For example, if the goal is for students to be able to do complex algebraic equations, the students need to understand the concept of order of operations, which is brackets, exponents, decimals, multiplication, addition, and subtraction (or BEDMAS). If we fail to differentiate by readiness, the students whose starting point is well below the benchmark will likely not move closer to that benchmark, but rather move further away from it.

Ruth Berry (2008), in her examination of teachers' beliefs about fairness, interviewed teachers' perceptions of fairness and categorized them according to several themes. First, teachers tend to equate fairness with all students doing the same work (Berry, 2008; Welch, 2000). According to Berry, in the interviews, teachers made comments such as "We need to be fair," "It's important to try to be fair," and "The teacher must treat everyone fairly." Also, teachers struggle with the perceived advantage they provide to those students who are permitted to do less or receive some type of modification or adaptation. Teachers were also concerned with students' perceptions of fairness (Berry, 2008). The notion of fairness was particularly relevant in the area of assessments. Teachers perceived adapting the assessment to students' readiness levels to offer those students an unfair advantage. Finally, teachers equated the concept of fairness in class to fairness outside of the classroom, such as during sports competitions (Berry, 2008, 2010). In sports competitions, then, this concept would have all students start on the same starting line because that is only fair. With this comparison, it became even further elucidating for teachers that certain students would have an unfair advantage if the teachers were to adapt the instruction according to different levels of readiness. It seemed unfair to them in the classroom, just as it seemed unfair on the sports field (Berry, 2008).

The problem with this notion of fairness and its interference with your ability to differentiate instruction and assessment seems to be a misunderstanding of the term *fairness*. Fairness does not mean equal. Fairness means everyone gets what he or she needs (Riordan, 2010). In order for students to succeed, which is our ultimate pursuit, they need to receive the instruction that will enable this to occur. Consequently, students will need to receive different levels and types of supports at different times, in different ways, and for different elements of the curriculum (Levy, 2008; Westwood, 2016). Not providing this would be unfair.

It's often a good idea to take the time at the start of the year to explain the concept of fairness and what it will look like in your classroom, because students' perceptions of fairness are likely based on what is most obvious to them: the amount of material required to complete or the length of the text to read in comparison to their classmates (Berry, 2008). However, teachers can educate students about the meaning of fairness, rather than respond to their developmentally appropriate but insufficiently developed notion of it.

One way to illustrate this could be to request that all students who are wearing glasses remove them. You can continue by stating that it would be "unfair" to allow only some students to wear glasses. Either all should wear them, or none should. This, of course, would seem unreasonable to the students—and they'd be right. It's unreasonable to suggest that students who need glasses should not wear them or that those who don't need them should. You could then explain that fairness means that each student has access to what he or she needs based on who he or she is. You could elaborate by explaining that the classroom will operate according to this notion of fairness, stating that you will do your best to meet individual needs throughout the year. Once said, this should not be an ongoing discussion. You could model fairness throughout the year, but try to avoid lengthy discussions each time you need to adapt work for certain students.

Teachers in differentiated classrooms need routines for addressing the inevitability that some students will be ready to move ahead in content, while others will need more time. Although there are many strategies to differentiate instruction, I will present the ones that are most effective in ensuring success for all students, according to teacher feedback I've received over the years, and the ones that are the most practical.

Differentiated Instruction and Universal Design for Teaching and Learning

A concept that teachers often confuse with differentiation is Universal Design for Teaching and Learning (UdL). UdL originated in the field of architecture (Mace, 1985). The idea is that prior to building any structure, architects must begin by considering the building's users and their needs (Hitchcock, Meyer, Rose, & Jackson, 2002). Who are they? What are their unique needs? For example, if architects build a new retirement home, they need to account for the diversity of individuals needing access to the building and build the structure to accommodate their needs. If not, there will likely need to be retrofitting later, to accommodate the needs of the users as an afterthought (Hitchcock et al., 2002; Stanford & Reeves, 2009). Elements added as an afterthought, such as a ramp for those in a wheelchair, will not be as effective and useful as those developed as part of the initial design. Retrofitting will sometimes occur in the case of an older building or a feature of the building that was not considered. It is often inevitable that some retrofitting will be needed, but the goal is to avoid it if at all possible.

Therefore, UdL is a paradigm that highlights the need to identify the users, think about their needs, focus on removing barriers (stairs), provide access (a ramp), and attempt to provide universal accommodations that everyone can access (Hitchcock et al., 2002). The concept of UdL was extrapolated from the field of architecture to the field of education (Rose, 2000; Rose & Meyer, 2002). The starting point is: Who are the users? What are their overall needs? What might be barriers to their learning? How do we remove the barriers and provide access?

There are many similarities between UdL and differentiated instruction. However, it is important to highlight how to integrate these two ideologies or paradigms into classroom teaching. First, the only way to meet student needs is to identify what those needs are. This is the first phase in differentiation as well as UdL. Therefore, at the start of each year, it's important to have a clear sense of who your students are (adolescents, students with limited English proficiency, or students with low reading levels) and what their general needs are (reading support, modified or adapted texts). These concepts are critical in both UdL and differentiation (Katz, 2013; Minarik & Lintner, 2011; Stanford & Reeves, 2009). UdL highlights the importance of getting to know the user or the learner (Meyer, Rose, & Gordon, 2016), whereas differentiation speaks of the unique needs of the students in terms of their interests, learning profile, and readiness levels (Tomlinson, 2014).

The next phase in the teaching process is to have clarity around the specific yearlong learning goals and to break them down into goals for the unit and the lesson. It isn't possible to meet individual needs without a clear sense of what the goals are. This concept relates to both UdL and differentiation (Katz, 2013; Minarik & Lintner, 2011; Stanford & Reeves, 2009). Authors Carol Ann Tomlinson and Jay McTighe (2006), in their book *Integrating Differentiated Instruction and Understanding by Design*, say that Understanding by Design (UbD) requires teachers to think deeply about content knowledge, authenticity, and meaning of the learning and behavioral outcomes that are clear and purposeful. As such, you become designers of your units, much like the architect according to the paradigm of UdL. Prior to meeting student needs, it's critical to highlight the expectations.

Differentiated instruction is also a complex process that highlights the need to identify student attributes and consider learning goals according to student needs. Flexibility and reflective practice are required in order for the designer to consider what worked and what needs to be adjusted (Tomlinson, 1999, 2001, 2014; Watts-Taffe et al., 2012). Therefore, in order to ascertain what students' needs are, it's important to identify the barriers that exist and the ways in which you can provide access.

Once you have articulated the learning goals, you can more easily identify potential barriers. For example, if the learning goal is to solve a multistep word problem, the text or word problem will be a barrier to a student with a reading challenge. Similarly, the word problem will likely also be a challenge for an English learner. In UdL, providing access by removing barriers is an essential concept. In the area of architectural design, a barrier would be the staircase, and access could be provided by building a ramp. Essential to the concept of UdL is that you must conceptualize the barrier in terms of an obstacle that can be removed. Therefore, it's far more effective if having poor organizational skills, ADHD, or a specific learning disability are not identified as barriers according to UdL, because these are conditions or disorders that are part of the individual and not qualities that can be easily remediated or removed. In order to provide access, you need to think of the barrier in terms of what can be altered or eliminated (Meyer et al., 2016; Tomlinson, 2014). The barriers that teachers can perhaps remove might be, for example, a forgotten textbook, a difficult text, or a lecture that is too long. Once you write the barriers in these terms, it is easier to imagine how you might remove or alter them in order to provide access (Hitchcock et al., 2002; Tomlinson, 2014). For example, having an extra set of textbooks in the classroom, increasing the time in which students are actively involved in learning, allowing the students to leave class a few times each period (for a short amount of time only), reducing the complexity of the text, or having the students read with a partner are all examples of ways in which you can provide access. Once you remove or alter these elements, the students can gain access, much like a ramp will allow the individual in a wheelchair to gain access to a building.

Rather than conceptualize UdL and differentiated instruction as two unrelated or contradictory paradigms, it is far more beneficial to identify the benefits of each one and incorporate the elements of both of these models to enrich teaching and learning in the diverse classroom. UdL has enlightened the field in terms of the focus on the user, barriers, providing access, and avoiding retrofitting, as well as the three ways in which student needs can be met (CAST, 2011; Rose, 2000). Differentiation has also enriched the field with its focus on the need to consider students' readiness levels, interests, and learning profiles, and by finding ways to meet those needs through differentiating by process, content, and product (Tomlinson, 2014).

Both differentiated instruction and UdL are paradigms replete with strategies to support student learning and ensure that you can remove barriers and provide access. For example, differentiated strategies include providing students with choice, differentiating by readiness using tiered learning, using individual contracts for students who are advanced, or using 2-5-8 menus to allow students to respond to questions at their level of proficiency. Some of these strategies will be discussed later in this chapter (see The Strategy, page 120), with concrete examples exemplifying how strategies may materialize in different unit topics.

It is important to note, however, that while proponents of differentiated instruction and UdL write a great deal about individual learning profiles, the evidence does not support the attainment of learning goals and overall success in school as a result of teaching according to student learning styles (Landrum & McDuffie, 2010).

⊕ THE STRATEGY

Given the importance of teaching to the diversity that exists in every classroom, Carol Ann Tomlinson (1999, 2001) identifies at least three ways in which teachers can address diversity: (1) differentiating by content, (2) differentiating by process, and (3) differentiating by product. This section will delve into each of these, presenting strategies for each. It will then offer several differentiation strategies using UdL, along with further differentiation strategies including anchor activities, tiered learning, 2-5-8, and tic-tac-toe.

THE IMPORTANCE OF CHALLENGING BELIEFS ABOUT DIFFERENTIATION

I was once leading a workshop on differentiated instruction for a group of thirty high school teachers. I began the session setting the foundation for differentiation and the dilemma that exists in all classrooms. When teachers focus on content at the expense of students—for example, by telling them "You have to complete chapter 3 by the end of the week"—only some of the students will successfully master the learning goals. Some others will likely struggle because of a gap in prerequisite knowledge or skills, and some others will have already mastered the material and will become bored with the instruction. Who would be satisfied to know that you focused on such a small portion of the students in your classroom? I continued to speak about the importance of providing students with opportunities to experience success, because only by experiencing success can students begin to envision themselves as capable learners (Ames, 1992; Bandura, 1986; Urdan & Schoenfelder, 2006).

Early on in the presentation, one teacher raised his hand. I saw from his expression that he was about to present me with a challenge. This was not a new occurrence. With years of experience, I have become familiar with many of the interjections that tend to occur, so I try to incorporate alternate perspectives and deeper explanations in areas that are likely to be controversial. However, this was a new one for me. The teacher, looking perplexed, asked, "Can't we just accept that some students will succeed and others won't?" I took a moment and then responded with "The greatest challenge, I believe, for any teacher is to see that student who was struggling finally succeed."

This belief is not uncommon. By far, one of the most significant challenges that teachers face each time they enter a classroom is the level of diversity that exists (Achinstein & Barrett, 2004). The creators of the school system and classroom curricula arbitrarily decided that students born within a certain time frame will learn together and accomplish the same goals in the same limited amount of time (Tomlinson, 2001); however, of course, this does not play out in the real-life classroom. You experience daily the challenges inherent in meeting diverse academic, behavioral, and social needs in the classroom (Tattoo, 1996; Tomlinson, 2001), but in order for change to occur, it's important for you to see yourself as the driving force behind the change.

Differentiating by Content

Differentiating by content refers to the strategy of providing students with curricular materials aimed at their unique levels, such as varied texts, supplementary notes for certain students, and supplementary materials provided as needed. Content consists of facts, concepts, generalizations or principles, attitudes, and skills related to the subject, as well as materials that represent those elements. Content includes both what you plan for students to learn and how the students can gain access to the desired knowledge, understanding, and skills. In many instances in a differentiated classroom, essential facts, material to be understood, and skills remain constant for all learners.

Differentiating by Process

Differentiating by process denotes the multitude of strategies that you can use to address the different readiness levels that are present in all classrooms, such as tiered instruction, cubing activities, and contracts developed between teacher and student. *Process* is how the learner comes to make sense of, understand, and own the key facts, concepts, generalizations, and skills of the subject. A teacher can differentiate an activity or process by, for example, providing varied options at differing levels of difficulty or based on differing student interests. A specific example of process is when a teacher decides to engage students in a jigsaw activity. A jigsaw strategy works best when material can be divided into chunks. In this case, the teacher might divide students into groups of four—called the *home group*—with each student in the group reading a different text detailing one of the four conditions in which the state might need to intervene in the lives of its citizens. Students would be asked to summarize the key points in their passage. Then, the students would form different groups according to the text that they read (for example, all of the students who read about a natural disaster occurring would meet together) into groups called *expert groups*. These expert groups would then share out their key points and add to their list if they omitted an important idea. Students would then return to their home groups, with individual students summarizing for the other members of their group the key elements of their reading passage. Teachers might choose this method as a teaching process because it enables students to be fully engaged in the learning, and the material (four categories) enables the use of this strategy.

Differentiating by Product

Another element of differentiation is that of *differentiating by product*. The term *product* is used to refer to ways in which a student can demonstrate what he or she has come to know, understand, and be able to do as the result of an extended period of study. A product can be, for example, a portfolio of student work; a research report; an information brochure; an exhibition of solutions to real-world problems that draw on knowledge, understanding, and skill achieved over the course of a semester; an end-of-unit project; the development of a Power-Point to teach a concept to your classmates; or a complex and challenging pencil-and-paper test. According to Tomlinson (1999, 2001, 2014), these different strategies for differentiating instruction are based on students' diverse readiness levels, interests, and learning styles.

Differentiating Using Universal Design for Learning and Teaching

UdL also addresses different ways in which students can be provided with access. In particular, UdL focuses on multiple means of presentation or representation, multiple means of action and expression, and multiple means of engagement (Rose & Meyer, 2002, 2006).

Multiple Means of Presentation or Representation

Multiple means of presentation of material refers to the ways in which a teacher can present information such as using visuals or representation such as using multimedia sources to represent an image or concept. For example, ensuring that students have access both visually (can see it) and cognitively (can process it) is of critical importance (CAST, 2011). For example, you can offer ways to display information so that it is visible and perceptible to all students, such as by altering the size of text, providing images or tables to support text, or speaking in a volume that allows all students to hear the information. The organization responsible for educating the public about UdL, CAST, provides a plethora of research positing the effectiveness of multiple forms of representation such as modifying text (Hughes & Wilkins, 2002) and incorporating multimedia sources into the learning experience (Schwan & Riempp, 2004).

In addition, you can enhance the representation of new information by accessing students' background knowledge (what they already know about the subject) and representing the material graphically (Venn diagrams or sequence charts) (CAST, 2011; Strangman, Vue, Hall, & Meyer, 2003). Teachers can also frontload vocabulary by presenting challenging vocabulary prior to introducing students to a difficult text or reading a text out loud for students who struggle to decode (CAST, 2011; Israel, Maynard, & Williamson, 2013). Table 6.1 (page 124) provides some examples of multiple means of presentation and representation.

Multiple Means of Action or Expression

Multiple means of action or expression refers to providing students with varying opportunities to show what they know (CAST, 2011). Students differ in the ways in which they navigate learning spaces. Therefore, in order for all students to have opportunities to express what they know, the pacing or timing in a classroom needs to take individual needs into account (CAST, 2011).

Oftentimes, the pacing of the classroom is too quick, thus not permitting certain students the opportunity to show what they've learned or where they are in the process of learning. For example, if students in a mathematics class are required to complete problems and have only a set amount of time before the example is shown to them on the board, some students will miss out on the opportunity to complete the examples on their own. Students who struggle to follow the steps in a procedure (for example, when solving an algebraic equation) could be provided with a checklist of steps.

Table 6.1: Multiple Means of Presentation and Representation

WHAT TO DO	HOW TO DO IT
Multiple Means of Presentation	
Alter size of text.	Use larger text and fewer words on a page for students who find the amount of text a barrier.
Provide images or tables.	Supply an image of a cell for all students or students who are supported by images and words.
Speak loudly and clearly.	
Speak slowly with frequent pauses.	Speak slowly for second-language learners.
Frontload vocabulary.	Teach students challenging vocabulary before they read these words in a text.
Multiple Means of Representation	
Incorporate multimedia sources.	Play a video clip showing the process of digestion.
Use a Venn diagram to represent information.	Compare two different habitats with a Venn diagram.

The use of graphic organizers is also a useful way for students to show what they know (Strangman et al., 2003). Some students who have difficulty expressing ideas linguistically might be far more proficient expressing themselves using graphic organizers. Here again, CAST cites researchers who have studied the effectiveness of using varying means of expression (Dye, 2000). Furthermore, students can show what they know by writing or typing alone or with a partner, or by creating a slideshow presentation with visuals to show what they've learned. Table 6.2 provides some examples of multiple means of action or expression.

Table 6.2: Multiple Means of Action or Expression

WHAT TO DO	HOW TO DO IT
Present material visually.	Include charts, lesson outlines, graphs, picture aids, and PowerPoints.
Include reading and writing.	Use books, texts, lesson outlines, dictionaries, and note-taking.
Lecture.	Give verbal instructions, hold discussions, create listening centers, hold Q&A sessions, and have students repeat the key points to friends.
Allow movement.	Incorporate body movement, touching, feeling, and hands-on learning.

Multiple Means of Engagement

Using multiple means of engagement is the final area CAST addresses. The focus is on engaging students in the learning by taking into account their varying interests, providing choices, and varying the level of challenge (CAST, 2011; Rose, 2000). Here again, differentiation incorporates these areas of student needs within its framework by acknowledging students' unique interests, readiness levels, and learning profiles. Ensuring that the work is authentic and valued, and that it resonates with the students by making it culturally relevant and age-appropriate, is an essential feature of instruction. For example, while some students are working on decoding activities, more advanced students can work on creating their own written text. To make this authentic, you can ask students to create texts that can be useful for other students in their classroom. Specifically, in one high school classroom there were students at significantly different reading levels, and there was a dearth of simple yet age-appropriate text for struggling high school readers. While weaker readers were working on simple decoding exercises, more advanced students were writing theme-based, age-appropriate, simple texts that the weaker students could read.

It is important that teachers minimize the level of threat in a classroom and to provide optimal levels of sensory stimulation (Brand & Dalton, 2012). All students need to feel like they can take risks and not be ridiculed by classmates who laugh at their incorrect responses.

An excellent exercise to introduce the concept of taking risks and not fearing an incorrect response is an activity conducted as a culmination of a unit or a section of a unit. Each student is presented with a random picture; for example, they could receive a picture of a suitcase, a dog, a painting, a potato chip, or a train. Students are asked to make a connection between the image and the current unit of study. For example, if a student receives a picture of a painting and the class is studying literary devices, the student might say that the colors in the painting make the image come to life just like literary devices do in a text. You could explain to your students that these are the types of activities that you will be engaging them in over the year—activities that do not focus on a correct response but rather activities that require creative thinking.

With regard to increased stimulation, the classroom can be structured such that if students need breaks, they can have a pass to leave the class, or if they need to stand at the back of the class, it is possible they can do that as well. I recall entering a classroom and being struck by a group of students standing at the back of the class with an ironing board as their desk. They needed to stand while learning, and the teacher found a marvelous way for them to do this.

In terms of authentic, meaningful, and purposeful learning and evaluations, researchers have written substantially about both differentiated instruction and the Universal Design models. Learners need to understand why they are learning what they are learning (know the learning goals). Real-life applications to learning situations should be applied as often as possible (CAST, 2011). For example, if students are learning about parabolas, the teacher can present them with an authentic task that requires them to become physics consultants hired by a film company on a film that includes many stunts. Understanding the science of parabolas and the angle of the stunt is critical if the stuntperson is to remain safe. Similarly, in an English language arts class focusing on the writing of letters, the unit can begin with a video showing students a social issue that requires their support. The focus is on the need to express their voice, and the letter writing is the way in which that can be accomplished. In other words, to engage students in the learning, purpose and meaning are essential. Table 6.3 presents some examples of multiple means of engagement.

Additional Differentiation Strategies

As mentioned at the start of this chapter, differentiation is a belief, and that belief centers on believing that students' various needs should be met within the context of the classroom. However, in order for those needs to be met, there are strategies or tactics that need to be applied. Examples of these strategies are anchor activities, tiered learning, 2-5-8, and tic-tac-toe.

Table 6.3: Multiple Means of Engagement

WHAT TO DO	HOW TO DO IT
Vary the readiness level.	Have some students who are working on decoding activities while others are creating their own text.
Provide meaning.	Begin with the KUD or learning goals so that students have a clear sense of what they will need to know by the end of the lesson, why they're learning what they are learning, and how they will need to show mastery.
Utilize authentic engagement.	In an English language arts class learning about expository writing, have students write letters or emails about a social issue and why it must be addressed with seriousness (for example, poverty or the environment). In a science class focusing on parabolas, students could take on the role of physics consultants working on a stunt for an action film.
Reduce the level of threat for fear of incorrect responding.	Engage students in activities where no correct answer is expected (for example, a connection between an image and the content).

Anchor Activities

It's never the case in any classroom that all students need exactly the same amount of time to achieve mastery in a particular area. *Anchor activities* are the key to effectively managing the differentiated classroom. An anchor activity is a task or set of tasks that students can go to when they complete an assignment (Tomlinson, 1999, 2001, 2014). It's best to tell students at the beginning of the school year that you will provide anchor activities for them to work on independently at the beginning of class or when they finish their assigned work. This frees you up to work with individuals or small groups of students who are struggling or simply need more time to complete assigned tasks. Meanwhile, the students who have mastered the content or skill work independently on different, more advanced tasks and activities that are engaging and stimulating.

The term *anchor activities* (Tomlinson, 2001, 2014) emanated from the concept of an anchor that temporarily holds a boat in place. You can keep file folders with anchor activities that are typically organized according to subject area, such as mathematics, science, or English language arts. When students complete their assigned work and are ready to move on to something more challenging, they can find this file folder and autonomously begin working on these extension activities. A well-managed system for anchor activities allows for different groupings based primarily on readiness or current level of mastery (Tomlinson, 2001, 2014). With this in action, students can be engaged in work rather than idly waiting for their classmates to complete their work.

Anchor activities can take one class period or can be ongoing. However, it is always important to ensure that the anchor activities are not busywork but rather opportunities for students to spend some time enriching their skills. The following section presents some examples according to subject area, and you can find many other examples of anchor activities online, but it is important to be critical when reading these examples to make sure that they serve their purpose and provide enrichment.

There are four things to consider when developing anchor activities. First, the anchor activities should comprise work that students can do independently so that you can work with students who may need guidance. Second, the activities should produce a visible output from students. For example, asking students to read without creating any written output is problematic as there is no evidence that the student is in fact engaged in work. Third, the anchor activities shouldn't be too much fun. It's important to keep in mind that while some students are working on their anchor activity, others are either working with the teacher or completing their work. Witnessing students engaged in activities such as using media to create videos or working on an art activity might discourage those trying to complete their work. Finally, it is best if students work individually, again, so that others can focus on completing their work or getting the guidance needed.

The following are examples of anchor activities that can be used within specific disciplines. While specific examples might not work in a specific classroom, the examples might lead teachers to think of other anchor activities that can be used.

LANGUAGE ARTS

- Write in a journal.
- Respond to the quote of the day.
- Read and respond to a biography or autobiography of an interesting personality.
- Write a letter to an author of a book you enjoyed.
- Write a story that combines two different genres about the same topic.

- Rewrite the ending of a book.

- Write a simple story using four words: *someone, wanted, but, so*.

- Create a dialogue between two characters in a novel.

- Write about what would have happened if . . .

- Write about your favorite food (justify your choice).

- Describe a picture using at least four figures of speech.

- Complete word puzzles to develop vocabulary words.

- Change the metaphors in a novel to similes.

- Add two examples of hyperbole or personification to a chapter in the novel.

The following are examples of anchor activities in a language arts class.

In a high school class, you are working on the structure of an expository text using an effective process of scaffolding. You ask your students to create a skeleton of a text they will be producing based on a specific structure presented. Some students will have an easier time with this than others, and the students who complete the task autonomously can then write a series of texts that you can use for younger grades. Once students feel ready to work on the skeleton, they return to their seats. Students who continue to struggle remain with the teacher. In most cases, it doesn't take too long before the students feel capable to work on their own.

In this activity, all students are required to attain the same learning goals, but some students are able to show what they know with fewer words or sentences. Inherent in this is the ability to reduce the complexity of the task for certain students.

In the primary grades, the focus is likely to be on reading. For example, you will likely be working on certain sound blends. You could introduce the blend, provide examples, role model, and ask students to individually identify words with the blend. You could then ask students to work on exercises solidifying this skill. Those who have completed the examples would move on to the anchor activity. In this case, the anchor could involve finding a partner and reading a text with vowel blends, or it could be done independently. If done with a partner, you could emphasize that students need to do the activity quietly to allow you to work with individual students or small groups. Those who are having difficulty would be working with you more directly, learning how to identify these blends.

MATHEMATICS

- Create test questions for the upcoming test.

- Create mathematics games.

- Research a mathematics topic.

- Create a bartering system for your town or city.

- Create a budget for an upcoming trip.

- Create a slideshow to effectively teach the new concept to an absent student.

- Write exam questions based on today's class.

- Write out the steps of the problem using images to support learning.

The following are examples of anchor activities in a mathematics class.

You begin by introducing a new mathematics concept using a real-life application and explicitly teaching the steps students require to effectively solve the problem. You use a scaffolding process to ensure that your students have at least a fundamental understanding of the steps and process and have had sufficient time to process the new information. Once your students have learned the process and steps, you provide them with examples to complete. Some of your students will be able to complete these examples with ease. Similar to the language arts example given previously (page 128), you could ask these students to create word problems highlighting specific skills. Additionally, you could ask these students to write out the steps that need to be followed for students who are struggling.

At this point, approximately two-thirds of your students will have completed the exercises proficiently. All students, except those who are struggling, are now working on anchor activities. The students who are struggling and have not yet mastered the skill are working with you at your desk or in some corner of the classroom. You might want to review the steps more explicitly, responding to questions that are troubling your students. One by one, your students will "get it" and return to their seats. Rather than work on the anchor activity, you could provide them with additional practice. If they get stuck, they are free to come back to the working corner and ask for clarification. The students are much freer and less intimidated to ask questions in this smaller group.

One of the most significant challenges students who struggle to achieve benchmark goals face is that school is moving too quickly for them (Wood, 2002). They haven't yet mastered a basic skill or subskill, yet you have already moved on to the next one. When they finally begin to master a basic skill, they don't have sufficient time to develop automaticity because the next skill, subskill, or content must be mastered (Tomlinson, 2014). Anchor activities are a highly effective mechanism to facilitate differentiated teaching because they provide enrichment for those who need it, freeing up the teacher to work with students who require one-on-one or small-group review (Tomlinson, 1999, 2001, 2014).

SCIENCE

- Create a review game.
- Write content songs.
- Write a biography of a scientist.
- Develop essential questions for the upcoming test.
- Create a mind map for a scientific concept.
- Write a list of the top ten environmental issues.
- Become the resident expert about a specific topic in science.
- Design an experiment.

HISTORY

- Create vocabulary flash cards.
- Develop a board game.
- Write a biography about a historical figure.
- Write a song about a difficult concept.
- Compare and contrast two meaningful historical events.
- Critique a political figure's platform.
- Write a journal of a day in the life of a historical figure.
- Find a song from each decade and explain how the historical context influenced the musician.

MUSIC

- Play piano with headphones.
- Create a new rhythmic pattern.
- Research a famous musician.
- Write a cantata.

ADDITIONAL EXAMPLES OF ANCHOR ACTIVITIES

The following anchor activities have academic value but don't necessarily need to be tied to a curricular unit.

- Create a comic strip for a book.
- Do an internet search and create a webpage on a topic of interest.
- Choose a historical figure, look up some key points, and generate a list

of questions you would ask that person.

- Summarize a current event article.

- Write an article for an ongoing class newspaper.

- Write a descriptive paragraph about anything in the classroom (for example, the colorful window shades).

- Generate a list of nouns, verbs, or adjectives that can be used for a spy novel.

- Turn a novel you are reading into a screenplay.

- Develop an anti-bullying curriculum.

- Develop "Would you rather . . . " statements such as, Would you rather have fought in the War of 1812 or the First World War? or Would you rather live in France or Britain?

- Develop a list of the most inspiring quotes to be used for public speaking competitions.

- Develop cartoons for daily news events.

Tiered Learning

Tiered learning is another effective tool that can and should be used in the differentiated classroom. To fully understand the concept of tiered learning, it's important to begin with an explanation of the concept of *flow*, introduced by Mihaly Csikszentmihalyi in 1990.

Csikszentmihalyi (2000), professor of psychology and management, best known for his research on the experience of flow, describes flow as the point where an individual performs at his or her most optimal level. For students to find flow, it means they have a feeling of complete immersion in an activity, where they're so engaged that their worries, sense of time, and self-consciousness seem to disappear (Csikszentmihalyi, 2000, 2014). Flow has been useful in understanding the importance of working within a suitable level of challenge. Think of it as "being in the zone," where time both speeds up and stands still.

Learning at its peak leaves the student in a state of flow. When in this state of flow, students are so completely immersed in the learning task that they lose all sense of space and time. When the school bell rings, it jolts them. In order to be in the state of flow, learners need to be engaged in work that is challenging but not to the level of anxiety (Csikszentmihalyi, 2000).

How, then, do you structure your classroom so that your students are working within their appropriate level of competency? The answer to this question points to *tiered learning*.

To answer the question as to how teachers develop differentiated expectations, it's useful to look at Bloom's revised taxonomy. Educational psychologist Benjamin Bloom created his taxonomy in 1956 to promote higher forms of thinking in education, such as analyzing and evaluating concepts, processes, procedures, and principles, rather than just remembering facts (rote learning) (Bloom, Englehart, Furst, Hill, & Krathwohl, 1956). It was most often used when designing educational, training, and learning processes. In 2001, educational psychologist Lorin Anderson, working with D. Krathwohl, published a revised taxonomy that showcases student actions versus nouns, as shown in figure 6.1 (Anderson et al., 2001). The updates are reflective of a more active thought process. Just like the original taxonomy, the revised version provides a valuable framework for teachers to use to focus on higher-order thinking.

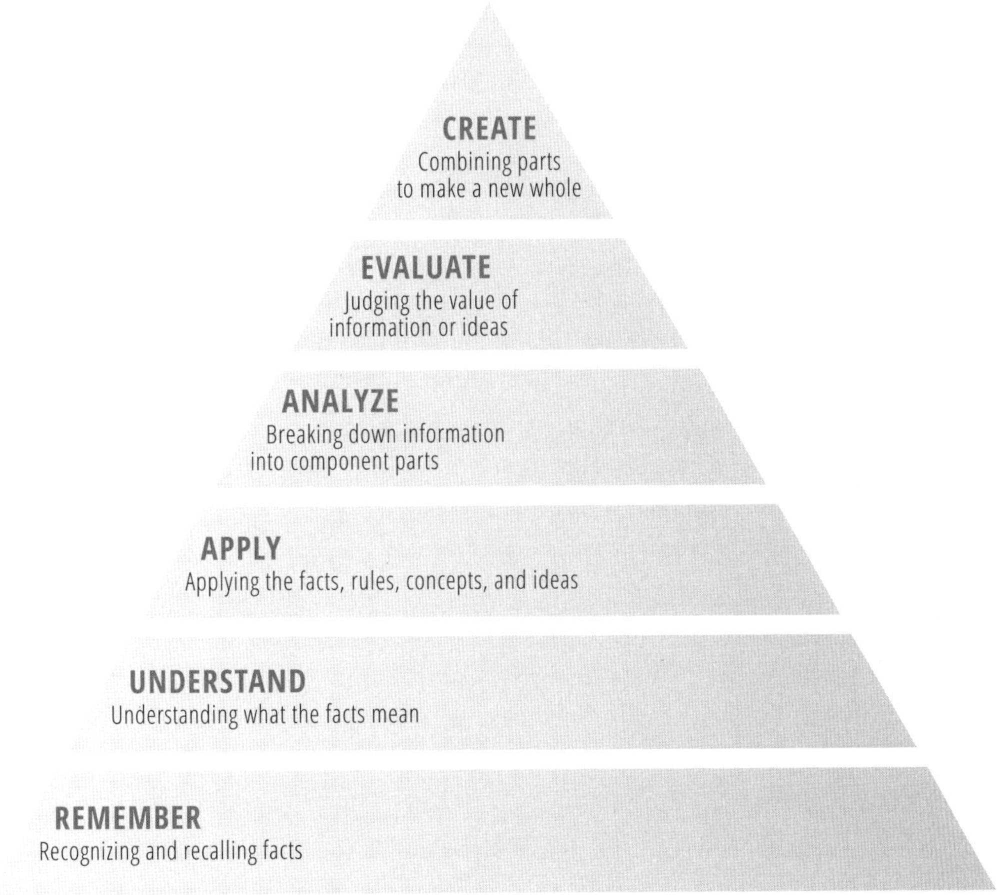

CREATE
Combining parts
to make a new whole

EVALUATE
Judging the value of
information or ideas

ANALYZE
Breaking down information
into component parts

APPLY
Applying the facts, rules, concepts, and ideas

UNDERSTAND
Understanding what the facts mean

REMEMBER
Recognizing and recalling facts

Source: Adapted from Anderson et al., 2001.

Figure 6.1: Bloom's revised taxonomy.

The revised taxonomy follows a trajectory from remembering to understanding, application, analysis, evaluation, and finally creation. Teachers can examine their learning goals for the day in light of this trajectory. If the goal for the day requires the student to engage in application (complete the mathematics equation), the students who are below grade level could be asked to engage in a task at a lower level of complexity—either remembering or understanding. For example, the focus could be on reviewing the necessary steps involved in problem solving or understanding the real-life application of the equation.

In order for students to maintain a level of flow at least some of the time, tiered assignments or activities developed using Bloom's revised taxonomy can be very effective. Williams (2002) notes:

> Tiered assignments are parallel tasks at varied levels of complexity, depth, and abstractness with various degrees of scaffolding, support, or direction. Students work on different levels of activities, all with the same essential understanding or goal in mind. Tiered assignments accommodate mainly differences in student readiness and performance levels and allow students to work toward a goal or objective at a level that builds on their prior knowledge and encourages continued growth. (as cited in University of Kansas, n.d.)

In order to create the optimal conditions for learning, you should offer learning challenges suited to each student's readiness level so that every student can learn in a state of relaxed alertness. Tiered instruction can help you create the conditions for students to work at their own pace and therefore maximize their potential to learn either by increasing their skill level with a given activity or by boosting the challenges they face (Levy, 2008; Tomlinson, 2014). As mentioned, every class is replete with students at diverse levels of readiness (Tomlinson et al., 2003), and so the old adage of aiming for the middle is not effective, as those on the perimeter will likely be left out.

To better understand tiered activities, let's use a sports metaphor. In a group of skiers, there will be those who have mastered parallel skiing, those who can go well beyond and ski on advanced moguls, and those who have just learned to ski down the beginner hill. Assume that the students who are parallel skiing are more or less at the same skill level; these students are the X group. Those who are advanced will be termed the X+ group, and those who have not yet mastered the learning goals—the beginner group—will be referred to as the X− students.

Let's assume that the learning goal for the day is for the students to ski down an intermediate hill using parallel skiing. Students are going to be evaluated on their ability to use techniques required of this level of skiing. If all students in this skiing group were required to master the same goals for the day, some would surely fall (and probably hurt themselves), and others would find this boring and lose interest quickly. Life for the ski instructor would be far easier if all students were at the same level of proficiency, but unfortunately that is rarely, if ever, the case. Therefore, you need to ask yourself the question, "What does the X– group of skiers need to learn in order to attain the learning goal, and what can the X+ students master, given that they have already mastered the goal?" Even in supposedly homogeneous groupings where students are grouped according to readiness level or ability, diversity exists as well. As long as there is more than one student in a classroom or group, diversity is going to be present; therefore, responding to this diversity is essential if our goal is effective student learning.

In a tiered classroom, it's important that you begin each lesson with an explicitly stated learning goal, knowing that you will provide several pathways for students to arrive at the objective. In this way, you can provide opportunities for your academically diverse students to learn at their current level.

The students who are able to master the goal with guidance from you, with help from their peers, or with in-class practice should be challenged at the X level. However, students who have not yet mastered essential prerequisite skills would need to develop those skills prior to being expected to master the learning goals. They would be working at an X– level. Those who have already mastered the learning goals for the day should be challenged at an appropriate X+ level.

Whenever I present tiered learning in a workshop, a common remark made by teachers is, "But there are end-of-year exams; there are standards students need to attain." While no one can dispute the responsibilities these standards place on you, this focus prioritizes qualified teaching over effective teaching, whereas you're trying to get to the point where *qualified* and *effective* intersect—the point where the focus is placed on the eventual success of the student knowing that of ultimate importance is his or her journey toward success rather than the year-end exams (Haycock, 1998, 2017).

I'm sure you entered the education field not only to succeed at teaching but also to see that all your students learn from you. What's the use of teaching to the standard if, at the end of the lesson or unit, student learning has not been fulfilled? A student can't be "willed" to succeed, nor can we expect our students to master lesson goals if they have not yet attained the prerequisite skills. A student with significant deficits in skill or knowledge who is continuously expected to master the learning goals will not likely move closer to the class goals. In fact, that student will more likely become frustrated and may even begin to feel like a constant failure, moving him or her further away from the learning goals. However, if an X–10 were given work at an X–8 level and had a taste of mastery, they would gradually move closer to the goal. Success breeds success, as it is motivating to want to keep achieving, but failure often begets greater failure and can cause students to retreat further away from even trying (Tomlinson & Moon, 2013).

The difference between what a learner can do without help and what the learner can do with assistance from peers or teachers, as introduced by psychologist Lev Vygotsky (1978), is known as the zone of proximal development. According to Vygotsky, learning is most effective when it's challenging enough for the student to succeed with the support of peers and teachers but not too challenging that the student will be unable to succeed even with some support. This refers to struggling students as much as it does to the students who have already mastered the goals (Vygotsky, 1978). In both cases, the students are working outside of their ZPD.

I'd like to propose that our task as educators is to increase the experiences of flow for students so that educators move from conversations on "student engagement" to conversations on flow. To do so, we need to begin with providing a classroom environment and structure that allows each student to learn within his or her ZPD.

Figures 6.2 through 6.7 (pages 136–140) provide some examples of tiered learning with learning goals across different content areas.

TOPIC OF STUDY: STARS AND CONSTELLATIONS	
KUD	**Learning Goal**
By the end of the lesson, students will know:	What a constellation is, names of constellations, and vocabulary used to explain constellations.
By the end of the lesson, students will understand that:	Constellations help us identify different groups of stars.
By the end of the lesson, students will be able to:	Write four facts about a specific constellation.
Level of Proficiency	**Learning Goal**
X	The same goal as identified above (the goal for the lesson): Write four facts about a specific constellation.
X–	Write out the definition of a constellation.
X+	Compare and contrast two of the constellations.

Figure 6.2: Examples of tiered learning with learning goals—science (stars and constellations).

TOPIC OF STUDY: ARGUMENTATIVE ESSAY WRITING	
KUD	**Learning Goal**
By the end of the lesson, students will know:	How to write an introduction for an argumentative essay; how to develop both sides of an argument.
By the end of the lesson, students will understand that:	An argumentative essay is meant to convince others of your point of view, and must therefore begin with strong, solid arguments.
By the end of the lesson, students will be able to:	Write an introduction, identify an argument and an opposing argument, and provide two facts for each side.
Level of Proficiency	**Learning Goal**
X	The same goal as identified above (the goal for the lesson): Write the introduction for your argumentative essay.
X–	Amongst the sentences listed below, which ones would you use for your introduction?
X+	Write out the ideas for your argumentative essay, based on your belief, then write an introduction for the opposing side.

Figure 6.3: Examples of tiered learning with learning goals—language arts.

TOPIC OF STUDY: STATES OF MATTER	
KUD	**Learning Goal**
By the end of the lesson, students will know:	The difference between solids, liquids, and gases.
By the end of the lesson, students will understand that:	Matter can be classified as a solid, a liquid, or a gas, and we can identify matter by its unique properties.
By the end of the lesson, students will be able to:	Draw a diagram of molecular structures for each state of matter.

Figure 6.4: Examples of tiered learning with learning goals—science (states of matter).

continued →

Level of Proficiency	Learning Goal
X	Provide two examples of solids, two examples of liquids, and two examples of gases. Choose one of the examples and draw a molecular diagram.
X–	From the list of items, identify whether each is a solid, liquid, or gas.
X+	Evaluate the following molecular diagrams of the two items and compare and contrast the molecular properties of each.

TOPIC OF STUDY: ANGLES	
KUD	**Learning Goal**
By the end of the lesson, students will know:	Terms associated with angles; how to compare angles; how to calculate the degree of certain angles.
By the end of the lesson, students will understand that:	Mathematical concepts such as angles can be represented symbolically. Once we are able to determine the most effective way to represent these concepts, we will have an easier time using these concepts in real-world applications, such as the building of bridges, navigation, or sports scenarios.
By the end of the lesson: students will be able to:	Construct angles using a protractor.
Level of Proficiency	**Learning Goal**
X	Construct angles using a protractor.
X–	Match the angle with the corresponding angle diagram.
X+	Create a design for a bridge using various angles.

Figure 6.5: Examples of tiered learning with learning goals—mathematics.

TOPIC OF STUDY: EXPLORATION	
KUD	**Learning Goal**
By the end of the lesson, students will know:	Names of explorers, key dates, contributions, and challenges.
By the end of the lesson, students will understand that:	Each explorer made a unique contribution to the new land, but it came with much conflict and challenge.
By the end of the lesson, students will be able to:	Explain each explorer's key contributions and challenges experienced.
Level of Proficiency	**Learning Goal**
X	Explain each explorer's key contributions and challenges experienced.
X–	Match each explorer with key contributions and challenges.
X+	Identify three of the most significant challenges of the explorers. If you were a consultant to the exploration at the time, what advice would you provide?

Figure 6.6: Examples of tiered learning with learning goals—social studies.

TOPIC OF STUDY: HELPING THE ENVIRONMENT BY REDUCING, REUSING, AND RECYCLING	
KUD	**Learning Goal**
By the end of the lesson, students will know:	The names of the 3 Rs (reduce, reuse, recycle).
By the end of the lesson, students will understand that:	We affect the environment in our daily lives with our actions and nonactions.
By the end of the lesson, students will be able to:	Apply the 3 Rs to your specific environment, and write about ways in which you can reduce, reuse, and recycle.

Figure 6.7: Examples of tiered learning with learning goals—science (recycling). *continued* →

Level of Proficiency	Learning Goal
X	Apply the 3 Rs to your specific environment, and write about ways in which you can reduce, reuse, and recycle.
X−	Match the action statements (such as "stop using straws") with one of the 3 Rs.
X+	Evaluate the benefits and costs of reducing, reusing, and recycling in your environment. How has it changed your environment? How might you convince others to do the same?

The 2-5-8 Strategy

Another strategy that you can use to differentiate instruction is 2-5-8 (Magner, 2000). It is a close relative of tiered learning, but unlike tiered learning, with 2-5-8 you encourage students to identify their comfort level or zone of proximal development rather than having the teacher decide for them as is done with tiered learning (Magner, 2000; Tomlinson, 2014).

Using Bloom's revised taxonomy, you can develop questions at different levels of complexity related to the content and learning goals for a particular lesson (Anderson et al., 2001). Each level is associated with a number: 2, 5, or 8. Remembering and understanding questions are worth two points, application and analysis questions are worth five points, and evaluation and creation questions are worth eight points (Hall, 2002; Tomlinson, 2014).

To utilize the 2-5-8 strategy, provide all the students with the same worksheet that has six two-point questions, three five-point questions, and two eight-point questions. (They won't need all the questions, but you provide extras at each level so they always have a choice regarding which questions they want to respond to.) Instruct students to respond to the questions that are most closely aligned with their level of mastery. If students feel as though they are just beginning to master the skills and content, they should answer the two-point questions. If they feel as though they have a solid mastery of the content, they should respond to the five-point questions, and if they believe that they have mastered the content and skill and require enrichment, they should respond to the eight-point questions. The weighting of the questions must equal 10. Therefore, students need to answer five of the two-point questions, two of the five-point questions, or one eight-point question plus one other question to meet the total (they are allowed to exceed 10 points). If students don't make choices that you feel are aligned with their current level, you can guide them toward more appropriate questions.

Using this approach enables students to respond to questions that are aligned with their level of mastery (Gregory & Chapman, 2012; Hall, 2002; Tomlinson, 2014). Furthermore, students who answer the two-point questions are able to linger longer on the more fundamental elements of content before moving on to application or more advanced questions.

To illustrate the point, figure 6.8 (page 142) contains examples of questions at each level.

It is important to keep in mind that as students move up the trajectory, the work that needs to be completed is less scripted with fewer, if any, parameters and more left up to the imagination of the student. Examples that might appear to be at a lower level (for example, the last example in the list of eight-point questions) are challenging when taking into consideration the age of the students. *A Taxonomy for Learning, Teaching, and Assessing* by Anderson et al. (2001) is a valuable resource on this topic.

Tic-Tac-Toe

Another activity allowing for differentiation is referred to as *tic-tac-toe* (Rutherford, 2008; Simpkins, Mastropieri, & Scruggs, 2009; Tomlinson & McTighe, 2006). Near the end of a unit, you can develop a tic-tac-toe matrix with nine different options for students to show what they have mastered up to that point in the unit. It's a great confidence builder as it provides them with choices as to how they would like to show mastery.

You can enhance student motivation with this activity by providing options whenever possible (Tomlinson, 2014; Tomlinson & McTighe, 2006). Offer an appropriate amount of choice so that students have a sense of autonomy and are able to choose an option that relates to their interests or readiness level while at the same time not facing an unlimited number of options. Figure 6.9 (page 142) shows a simple yet effective template that can be developed with ease and completed effectively by your students (Tomlinson, 2014; Tomlinson & McTighe, 2006). The tic-tac-toe method is a straightforward way to provide students with choice. Develop up to nine options or tasks presented in the format of a 3 × 3 matrix. For younger children, or in cases where it is preferable to have fewer choices, provide a smaller matrix.

Examples of Two-Point Questions	Examples of Five-Point Questions	Examples of Eight-Point Questions
• Define *mean, median,* and *mode.* • List the physiographic regions in North America. • Locate cities or capital cities, oceans, and seas on a map. • List the 3 Rs. • Define the terms *values, facts, opinion, digestion,* and *nutrients.* • List the parts of the digestive system. • List the stages of the water cycle. • Write the definition of *mitosis.* • Draw the life cycle of a plant. • Explain the terms *prime number* and *composite number* and provide two examples of each. • Explain how carbohydrates and proteins break down in the body. • Given a list of foods, indicate whether each one is a carbohydrate, fat, or protein. • Name three habitats. • Identify the first and last letter in a word.	• Design a graph listing the statistics of a sports team. • Sketch out a chapter in a novel. • Identify which articles can and cannot be recycled. • Write a quiz that a teacher can use to assess your knowledge of the life cycle. • Find examples of fractions in the newspaper. • Create a rule card that explains order of operations. • Convert ten fractions listed in your textbook to decimals and explain how you did it. • Provide an example of a balanced breakfast, lunch, and dinner. • Explain why we need to digest our food. • Match the animal to its habitat.	• Write a screenplay for a chapter in a novel. • Create a product that would meet specific criteria. • Develop a survey on eating preferences. • Create a video explaining the need for fractions to a group of fourth-grade students. • Write a speech espousing your beliefs and values, stating facts about the current situation in your district, city, province, state, or county, and opinions that you hold about the current situation. • Design a public service announcement that provides key information to the general public about healthy eating. • Write two sentences that explain why animals need to live in specific habitats.

Figure 6.8: Examples of 2-5-8 questions.

Task A	Task B	Task C
Task D	**Compulsory task**	Task E
Task F	Task G	Task H

Figure 6.9: Sample tic-tac-toe matrix.

You may decide that all students must complete at least one compulsory task, typically placed in the center square. Then, write eight additional tasks in the remaining squares. Instruct students to complete any line of tasks, as long as it crosses the center. For example, students can complete tasks A and H, F and C, D and E, or B and G, because all of these tasks cross the center task. You can place the tasks strategically according to interest. In designing tasks by interest, each diagonal line could represent a task that highlights a particular way of responding.

The tic-tac-toe format allows students to choose activities that are the best reflection of their current mastery level and abilities, while also allowing you to differentiate instruction for diverse learners (Dotger & Causton-Theoharis, 2010; Gardner, 1983; Tomlinson, 2014). The tasks listed on the matrix could be based on similar levels of challenge but provide different options for showing mastery—for example, "Create a PowerPoint" and "Create a board game" both intend to teach a group of students studying the current topic. Other examples include items like creating a timeline, analyzing a primary source, creating a jingle for a difficult concept, and preparing for a debate on an essential question.

Alternatively, you could arrange tasks on each of the rows according to readiness level. For example, row A could be the most basic requirements, row B could include requirements at grade level, and row C could have requirements listed above grade level. Keep in mind that tasks should not require students to do more of what they have indicated they are already capable of doing (Tomlinson, 2014). If a child has mastered addition of fractions with mixed numerals, the C-level task should not be based on more examples of the same concept. Students should be asked to go to the next level, in which they develop real-life applications of the concepts presented. Similarly, students who are either at or below grade level should be given tasks that are engaging and will lead them to meet the requirement. If a student is not yet capable of adding fractions with mixed numerals, for example, she could work on mastering the prerequisite task of adding fractions. Once she masters this, she should be able to complete a more challenging task. Using this example, the tic-tac-toe would be differentiated by both readiness as well as choice. Students would have three options within each readiness level to choose from.

Tic-tac-toe boards are an excellent strategy that provide students with choice and therefore enhance their motivation. Providing students with choice allows them to be in control of their learning and choose work that is aligned with their interests and level of readiness, and this enhances their sense of competence (Tomlinson, 2014; Tomlinson & McTighe, 2006).

Researchers explain that when students are externally controlled or given a task that they must complete and are provided with reinforcement for that task, there are fewer benefits than when a student is reinforced for a self-initiated task or activity (Brooks & Young, 2011; Deci, Eghrari, Patrick, & Leone, 1994;

Deci & Ryan, 2010). When students are able to choose the task, the result is a far more pronounced sense of competence and intrinsic motivation (Deci et al., 1994). According to other researchers, having choice is related to both increased motivation and increased performance outcomes (Alamri, Lowell, Watson, & Watson, 2020; Brennan, 2019; Cordova & Lepper, 1996). In order for choice to have maximum benefit, the choices you offer to the students must enhance their autonomy and must relate to their interests, goals, or culture (Katz & Assor, 2006). When you give students tasks or assignments within their ZPD, their sense of self-efficacy and motivation increases. In contrast, if the task is outside of the students' ZPD, either because it's too challenging or because it's too simple, the students are unlikely to feel competent or motivated (Vygotsky, 1978). The results of unfulfilled challenge are no less serious than the consequences for children who are given work that is too difficult.

Have you ever bumped into a former student who shared an experience he or she had in your classroom with you that you didn't even remember? They may have thanked you for your kindness, or a much-needed pat on the back, or constructive feedback that stayed with them all these years later. Often, it's the little things that make the biggest difference.

Figures 6.10, 6.11, and 6.12 provide some sample tic-tac-toe templates across different content areas.

Create a limerick to remind yourself of the order of operations.	Create word problems that include dividing fractions.	Provide two examples of when you would use fractions in the real world.
Illustrate a book of multiplication word problems.	Complete the multiplication word problems on the sheet.	Create a multiplication game to teach next year's students about multiplication.
Walk around the school and find three examples of fractions.	Make a book of multiplication word problems. Include all the vocabulary words related to multiplication.	Create a mathematics rap or poem to learn the process of dividing fractions.

Figure 6.10: Mathematics tic-tac-toe examples for various topics.

You are a documentarian who is recording the events that transpired during the time in which the novel took place.	You are a screenwriter who has been asked to turn the historical novel into a film. Begin with the first chapter.	You are a songwriter who is inspired by the novel. Write a song to depict the historical period.
You are a talk show host. Next week's show highlights the historical period depicted in the novel. Who will you invite? What questions will you ask your guests?	Novel study: Choose a novel that depicts a historical period. After reading the first chapter, write a summary of the historical period depicted in the novel.	You are a historian who has been asked to create a museum depicting the time period and events that transpired. Design the museum.
You are a critic at an agency who has been asked to write a critique article of the novel's depiction of the historical period.	Write out an interview between two characters in history depicted in the novel.	You are a set designer for an upcoming film. How will you design the sets for each scene? Make sure that the historical time period is accurate.

Figure 6.11: History/language arts tic-tac-toe.

Perform a thirty-second radio advertisement to encourage people to use oxymorons when they talk.	Perform a one-minute puppet show that teaches about apostrophes.	Make a WANTED poster using at least two metaphors. Include a picture.	Write a letter to a friend using at least five different kinds of figurative language in the text.
Interview an idiom of your choosing and write the transcript of the interview.	Create at least four newspaper headlines using an oxymoron in each.	Create a picture dictionary for these terms: *idiom*, *simile*, *metaphor*, *paradox*, *personification*, *oxymoron*, and *apostrophe*.	Write at least three jokes or puns using one kind of figurative language in each.

Figure 6.12: Language arts tic-tac-toe.

continued →

Make a comic strip with three characters using different kinds of figurative language.	Write a short story about a homework machine. Include one simile, one personification, and one metaphor.	Make a Venn diagram that compares and contrasts metaphors and similes. Write at least three sentences to summarize the diagram.	Create a set of six idiom flash cards. Be sure to include the answers on the backs of the cards.
Write one scene of a play that shows personification for at least three characters.	Act out four figurative language terms for a friend. Have your friend guess the terms you are acting out.	Create your own crossword puzzle that includes these terms: *idiom, simile, oxymoron, metaphor, personification, paradox,* and *apostrophe.*	Create three mathematics story problems for others to solve using a different figurative language descriptor in each problem.

There is an overabundance of differentiation strategies that you can access to bring your value as a teacher to fruition. You just need to remind yourself why you're in this. You need to commit and recommit, especially when feeling disillusioned, to using different strategies that are there to help ease the task of delivering the best you can to your students.

⌐ NEXT STEPS

Identify one strategy to implement each month. As you try out each new strategy, remember to write a reflection so that you can use that information the next time you try out the strategy. For example, you might note that when you try the tic-tac-toe strategy for the first time, the activities in each of the squares are too complex; thus, next time you may need to lessen the complexity of each one. Or you might note that some of the activities take much longer to complete than others, or that some of the activities don't address the learning goals. You will also want to keep a record of the success of the implementation. Your written reflections will enable you to keep a log of the successes and perhaps modifications you'd like to make in the future.

The reproducibles on pages 147–150 provide templates for some of the strategies presented in this chapter. I suggest that you begin with tic-tac-toe, then move to 2-5-8, anchor activity, and finally tiered learning due to the level of complexity of each of these strategies.

Tic-Tac-Toe Template

Reflections:		

2-5-8 Template

Two-point questions	Five-point questions	Eight-point questions
(Total of six questions so that students who choose these questions will be able to respond to five of the six questions below to equal 10)	(Total of three questions so that students who choose these questions can respond to two of the three questions below to equal 10)	(Total of two questions so that students who choose these questions can respond to one of the two questions below plus any other question on the sheet for a total of 10 or more)
Reflections:		

Anchor Activity Template

Classroom activity to develop the learning goals. (Here some students are going to require more time to complete the activity.)	Anchor activity for students who completed their work	Small-group instruction for students who are struggling to complete the activity
Reflections:		

Tiered Learning Template

PROFICIENCY LEVEL X	PROFICIENCY LEVEL X+	PROFICIENCY LEVEL X−
Most students should be able to master these learning goals.	Given that some students have already shown mastery of the X-level, they are now able to work on the following:	In order for students to master the X-level, they need to first master the following skills/subskills/content:

By the end of the lesson, students will

Know:

Understand:

Do:

By the end of the lesson, students will

Know:

Understand:

Do:

By the end of the lesson, students will

Know:

Understand:

Do:

Teaching With Purpose © 2021 Solution Tree Press • SolutionTree.com

Visit **go.SolutionTree.com/instruction** to download this free reproducible.

Developing Grit and Perseverance in Yourself and in Your Students

Are you unwavering in seeing your goals and objectives through? Are you mindful of your preparedness for class, of how you present yourself and your course material to the students? Do you live up to your commitments as a teacher? A large part of being purposeful in your teaching is bringing awareness to what is happening both within you and around you. It's about bringing yourself wholly and completely to the classroom and being attuned to your students' needs. As well, a part of being purposeful in your role as a teacher involves being aware of the complexities in the learning environment but not allowing obstacles or challenges to defeat you. It's about being compassionate, nonjudgmental, and patient while making the best example of yourself for your students so you set them up for success.

The purposeful teacher is fully prepared and present and does the best he or she can on every given day. It's a tall order, I know.

According to a plethora of research, the drive to serve our students purposefully requires us to develop *stickwithitness*, not only within ourselves but within our students as well. Stickwithitness is the ability to keep on going especially in the face of challenge (Duckworth, Peterson, Matthews, & Kelly, 2007; Hoerr, 2013). This concept of taking what we know and putting it into action, of sticking with it no matter how hard we might find things, has been titled *grit* and *perseverance*.

⚡ THE CHALLENGE

Far too often we use the word *lazy* to describe a student who doesn't seem to want to work—or to persevere in his or her work. But the problem with this is that it doesn't get us anywhere in our task to reach those particular students who appear to fall into this category. Referring to a student as lazy seems to symbolize a dead end. Furthermore, once a student is labeled as lazy, he or she will know it, and eventually will grow into the label in an even more pronounced way.

Also, as teachers, of course we want to believe in the success of all students, especially those who appear so difficult to teach (Ames, 1990; Kiefer et al., 2015). When we have the mindset that a student is lazy, it denotes a state that is constant and likely to stick to the child, because this conviction is invariably being communicated either explicitly or tacitly to the student (Bucholz & Sheffler, 2009; Dweck, 2006, 2007; Furrer et al., 2014). Instead, if we believe that lack of success is only temporary and that with hard work and effort, the student can gain mastery and achieve effective results, the "unmotivated" student is more likely to become motivated (Dweck, 2006, 2007). Couple this with a student who perceives poor performance on a test as a temporary setback due to some external circumstance rather than an "I'm so dumb" concept of the poor performance, and this becomes the fertile soil upon which grit and perseverance grow.

Of significant importance is the attributions that students make for their successes and failures. Their mindset related to this will have great influence over their short- and long-term success. If students believe that success is within their grasp, and that with effort success will ensue, they are far more likely to persevere in the face of challenge.

Attribution Theory to Understand Perseverance

The theory of attributions and the ways in which attributions are developed are useful when illustrating the problem with a lack of grit and perseverance in students. To study this theory, we will consider three separate cases or vignettes.

Case 1

Imagine a student who does very well academically. Now imagine that this same student, who always does well on all evaluations, performs poorly on a test. If a teacher asks what went wrong, the student will likely provide healthy attributions—attributions that are not constant and don't represent anything internally "wrong" with him or her. The student might respond with comments such as "I didn't know you were going to ask us questions on chapter 3" or "I had a lot of tests that week and didn't have enough time to study for all of them." These comments reflect that the student is aware of what got in the way and will likely do better next time.

Case 2

Conversely, if a student has a history of failing and fails yet another test, he or she is likely to self-blame. When asked what went wrong and why he or she failed, the student might say, "I'm dumb. I suck. I'll never get it," or at least feel that the failure is a result of his or her inability. These attributions are internal—in other words, very difficult to alter. Furthermore, these attributions are constant and lead the student to believe that he or she will do as poorly next time as he or she did this time.

Case 3

This one is perhaps the most interesting. If a student who has a history of failure does well on an evaluation and is asked by his teacher what he did that resulted in him doing so well, the most common answer will be luck. In other words, the stars were aligned in a certain way in the stratosphere. If the student is not able to identify what led to his success, he is likely not going to be able to repeat it in the future (Schunk, Meece, & Pintrich, 2008; Seifert, 2004; Weiner, 1972).

The different types of attributions that students choose regarding the causes of their action (or inaction) are descriptive of their motivations (or lack thereof) and impact their future behaviors in predictable ways. Therefore, if we don't teach students, especially those who have a long history of failure, the skills needed to attain success, they will unfortunately be doomed to continued failure (Hoerr, 2013).

Mindset Matters With Regard to Perseverance

Dweck (2006, 2007) determines how individuals respond to setbacks and failure when pursuing their goals. Those who are supported in embracing the struggle learn from it and keep moving forward; they persevere. Teachers with a fixed mindset believe that only some students are capable and likely to succeed, and in fact almost always do (Dweck, 2014a). Their success is viewed in terms of both the long term ("The student will do very well in mathematics this year") and the short term ("The student will do very well on this mathematics test"). Of course, the belief is not fabricated from thin air, but rather is often based on previous records, other teachers' input, and the current year's marks.

The problem here is a chicken-and-egg one. There is no doubt that previous data are important, and certainly that data will inform instruction. When educators use data, past and present, to the detriment of the student, this use of data becomes problematic. Inevitably, some students will struggle in mathematics, science, reading, and other areas, but your belief about their capacity will either negatively or positively influence their success (Dweck, 2014b). Students, especially the ones who struggle, are highly sensitive to your impressions of them (Furrer et al., 2014). They look for signs all the time—Does she think I'm capable, or does she think I'm going to fail? They see themselves in our reflection of them and often want to live up, or down, to the expectations that we hold of them. Furthermore, when you believe that a student's success or failure is fixed, you're likely to interact with the student accordingly. If you believe that students are not likely to succeed, your efforts and perhaps even unconscious interactions with them will reflect your expectations of them. The classroom as a healthy ecosystem requires that students see failure as a part of learning and believe, as a result of your actions and your overall demeanor, that you see them as successful learners. As a result, they will view one another in this positive light. Perseverance is a disposition that must be established through lots of experience and reinforcement (Hochanadel & Finamore, 2015). Above all, you need to remember that the most challenging students are the most vulnerable and the most desperate for your belief in them.

A growth mindset, on the other hand, is one that asserts that while the student hasn't passed the test today, with support, that student will likely pass it tomorrow (Dweck, 2006). A growth mindset sees students' success as malleable and subject to hard work and effective teaching. In other words, with a growth mindset, the teacher and student have far more control over their success in the future. Therefore, in order for students to strengthen their capacity for grit and persevere to consistently put forth substantial effort in the pursuit of success, both the teacher and the student must hold a growth mindset (Dweck, 2014a).

What this looks like in a classroom is fascinating. Imagine two students faced with a challenging mathematics problem, both at the same readiness level in terms of their understanding of mathematical concepts and, in particular, at the same level of understanding with regard to the concept with which they are engaging. One child begins to work, reads the problem, and immediately raises a hand. When the teacher approaches, the student says, "I don't know what to do." The teacher provides the first step in the process and then moves away. The child looks around for a few moments and then raises a hand again. This time the student states, with more agitation, "I can't do this problem." In contrast, there is another student who has the same mathematics problem to solve. This student begins and struggles at first but remains calm. The student looks around, seemingly wanting to ask for help, but instead begins working on the problem one step at a time. The second student is clearly developing more perseverance than the first. This principle is less about getting the correct response and more about developing the internal stickwithitness that counts.

✤ THE PRINCIPLE

In her research, Angela Duckworth (2007), University of Pennsylvania professor, defines *grit* as "passion and perseverance for long-term goals" (Duckworth et al., p. 1087). Grit entails working strenuously toward challenges and maintaining effort and interest over years despite failure, adversity, and plateaus in progress. Apart from instructing content of knowledge and facts, we need to provide opportunities for our students to develop noncognitive competencies such as grit, perseverance, and tenacity so that those who tend to give up easily don't. The gritty individual approaches achievement as a marathon; his or her advantage is stamina. Do you have it as a teacher? And how can you set the conditions for grit in students? What can educators do to prepare children and adolescents to thrive in the long term? And how do teachers motivate the difficult-to-motivate student?

Perkins's research proposes a theory of thinking based on dispositions (Perkins, Jay, & Tishman, 1993; Perkins, Tishman, Ritchhart, Donis, & Andrade, 2000) rather than ability, and is highly informative in presenting the importance of what he terms *dispositional factors* that result in a person's overall intelligent behavior, challenging the traditional notion of intelligence promulgated by Spearman (1904) and Binet and Simon (1961). Perkins et al. (1993) examined three factors in their research that result in an individual's overall intelligent behavior: (1) inclination, (2) sensitivity, and (3) ability.

Inclination refers to one's motivation and tendency "to invest mental energy" in a behavior. For example, Perkins and his colleagues (1993) provide an example of one's inclination toward being open-minded and will notice that is necessary in particular situations. *Sensitivity* denotes one's ability to exhibit awareness of the occasion to engage in a behavior. For example, to continue with Perkins and colleagues' example, those with an inclination toward open-mindedness will be more likely to use this disposition in situations that call for its use. Finally, *ability* is the basic capacity to carry out a behavior, or one's behavior not only to notice that open-mindedness is needed but to implement it when required as well (Perkins et al., 1993). Challenge the learner's cognitive bias and provide the learner with opportunities to acquire the basic capacity to become invested in his or her own learning, and the learner will develop the grit to persevere and override his or her attributions or challenging beliefs (Duckworth et al., 2007; Perkins et al., 1993).

Perkins and Tishman (2001) examined thinking dispositions of sensitivity, inclination, and ability to close the gap between what people are capable of doing and what they actually choose to do. As they articulately state, "The concept of thinking dispositions has been advanced as an explanatory construct that addresses the gap between ability and performance by identifying characterological traits, beyond or in addition to basic intellectual capacity, that are needed to mobilize ability" (Perkins & Tishman, 2001, p. 258).

Perkins was interested in the individual's ability to focus on the other side of an argument. In what he termed *confirmatory bias* or *myside bias*, his research showed the tendency to favor information that confirms attributed beliefs or ideas (as cited in Baron, 2000). Learners display this bias when they gather or remember information selectively, or when they interpret it in a biased way.

Intelligence, while it might assess what an individual is capable of doing, does not evaluate what individuals are likely to do. Perkins noted that "individuals with a high IQ were not more likely to attend to the other side of the argument than those with lower IQs" (Perkins, Farady, & Bushey, 1991, as cited by Perkins & Tishman, 2001, p. 2). The research is fascinating because for years, there seemed to have been an *X factor* or missing link in education, as was pointed out by Angela Duckworth (Duckworth, Quinn, Lynam, Loeber, & Stouthamer-Loeber, 2011). Why is it that some students with very high IQs do poorly, and some with lower IQs do so well? According to Perkins et al. (1993), Duckworth et al. (2007), and Dweck (2010), the concept of *stickwithitness* (to stick with the task at hand), effort, perseverance, or inclination is essential to student success but so undervalued in the educational system. It's possible that stickwithitness and other qualities like it are undervalued because they are not considered important to teach as with other standardized course material—and perhaps because the question then becomes "Is this something that can even be taught?" In theory, this intervention can change students' grit levels by changing their beliefs (Duckworth et al., 2011). Angela Duckworth is onto something that we, as educators, can use to elevate the effectiveness of how we teach and what they learn, so let's take a closer look at her key points regarding grit.

Grit is about developing clarity of purpose and direction, pursuing the chosen objective with a ferocious determination, hard work, and resilience. Duckworth's (2016) construct of grit is a combination of four elements.

1. **Passion:** Being interested in what we do and loving it to the core.

2. **Perseverance:** Engaging in determined practice—focused, full-hearted, challenge-exceeding practice, following the mantra of "whatever it takes" and daily discipline of doing it to get better and better.

3. **Purpose:** Being able to see and pursue the integral connection of one's work with others' well-being in the larger realm.

4. **Hope:** Rising-to-the-occasion kind of perseverance. Some of us are born with an inherent tendency for hope, a "sunny disposition." Others can consciously practice a hopeful view. Hope happens at all stages of gritty pursuits, not necessarily the last and final stage.

Within a standardized system of mastery, student grades become the marker of success (Perkins et al., 1993). An A is of higher value than a B. But the scores themselves don't tell the full story, nor do they indicate the extent to which students persevere in order to achieve a certain grade. Cognitively, they see a "role of evolving conceptual frameworks in cognitive change" (Perkins et al., 1993, p. 15), at least in the development of *thinking dispositions*, or *dispositions for good thinking* (what we might call critical thinking). As learners develop an increasingly sophisticated theory of mind, they develop the "conceptual developmental capacity to conceive of the mind as actively interacting with information" (Perkins et al., 1993, p. 15). "This move toward an active understanding of mind, is crucial to the development of virtually all the thinking dispositions" (Perkins et al., 1993, p. 30).

The interplay between the extrinsic forces and the intrinsic motives inherent in human behavior is the territory of self-determination theory. Researchers studying the theory of self-determination posit that the three fundamental needs underlying an individual's intrinsic motivation are autonomy, competence, and relatedness (Deci, 1971; Deci & Ryan, 2002, 2011), and that providing the social context to satisfy these needs will enhance intrinsic motivation (Ryan & Deci, 2000). External factors such as evaluations, reward systems, and opinions play a role, and so do internal motivations such as passions, habits, and curiosity, which are not necessarily externally rewarded or supported but can nonetheless sustain efforts and interest (Perkins et al., 1993). Self-determination theory sheds light on the role of choice in the classroom.

Of course, this all sounds very logical. After all, who could challenge the fact that students need to be motivated in order to learn, and be able to work autonomously and develop a sense of competence that will inevitably lead to a belief in their own self-efficacy? But again, how can teachers turn that unmotivated student into a student who wants to engage in even the most challenging tasks?

⊕ THE STRATEGY

We can't *will* students to succeed, but we can teach them how. Therefore, another condition essential to enhancing the grit to persevere is the necessity to provide students with the skills enabling them to do so (Duckworth, Akerman, MacGregor, Salter, & Vorhaus, 2009). Students need to be presented with a challenging goal, but one that is within their grasp, and we need to teach them how to reach that goal and stick with it in the face of inevitable setbacks.

Three elements are essential for the growth and development of perseverance: (1) equipping students with the skills and procedures that will enable them to persevere; (2) teaching students how to become autonomous in their actions, especially when they struggle; and (3) reinforcing all efforts toward developing grit and perseverance. These three elements are described in the following sections. Finally, we will discuss the strategies of designing tasks to elicit flow and valuing quality over quantity.

Equip Students With the Skills and Procedures That Will Enable Them to Persevere

First, students need skills and procedures to pursue (Zimmerman, 1989, 2002, 2013). For example, if we want students to understand what they are reading and to enjoy the book, they need a text that engages them as well as having strategies that they can apply in order to understand what they are reading. For example, reciprocal teaching, which includes questioning, summarizing, clarifying, and predicting, has been touted as one of the most effective comprehension strategies (Hattie, 2008). The Peer Assisted Learning System, or PALS (Chard, Vaughn, & Tylcr, 2002; Fuchs, Fuchs, & Burish, 2000), is another effective comprehension strategy that guides students to identify the verb of each sentence, then the noun (referred to as the who or the what of the sentence), and then to identify two important points about the who or the what. Effective instructional practice includes naming the strategy (reciprocal teaching or PALS), explicitly teaching students how to apply the strategy while reading a text through a *think-aloud*, during which you would list the steps in the strategy, then provide students with many opportunities to practice the strategy and reinforce them each time they do. Without these necessary skills, the students simply don't have the chance to develop grit and perseverance.

THE IMPORTANCE OF PROVIDING STUDENTS WITH STRATEGIES

The teacher of a second language in a high school class for students who have learning challenges asked her students to read a short story but failed to provide the necessary strategies they needed to engage in the task. Chaos ensued as the students argued with the teacher or roamed around the classroom trying to avoid doing the work. One student was sitting in his seat looking bewildered but seemingly willing to accept guidance. I sat next to him and showed him how to glean information from a text by following a PALS procedure (Chard et al., 2002; Fuchs et al., 2000) of reading the story and identifying the who or the what (the subject of each sentence) and one important fact about the who or the what. We read sentence by sentence and followed this pattern. As we progressed, the process became easier, and eventually he was working with very little guidance from me.

The bell rang, and all of the other students, who had not begun to work, charged out of the classroom. However, the student with whom I was working did not seem to hear the bell ring and continued to read each sentence using the strategy presented until the end of the story. The teacher later mentioned that this student was one of the most challenged students in the classroom. Yet, when he was equipped with the skills to succeed, he found he could do the task, and he became engrossed in the work.

Students must be shown strategies or the "how to" in order to succeed. "How to" typically involves a series of steps to follow. It is not sufficient to tell students what they need to do; rather, we need to show them how to do it through a process of modeling (Blackwell et al., 2014; Bucholz & Sheffler, 2009; Kiefer et al., 2015; Marzano & Marzano, 2001; van de Pol et al., 2010).

Teach Students Autonomy

The second condition that is essential if students are to become perseverant is the development of autonomy (Guay, Ratelle, & Chanal, 2008; Reeve, Ryan, Deci, & Jang, 2008). Once students have been shown how to do a task and an effective process of modeling has occurred ("I do, we do, you do one, you do many"), the teacher needs to allow students to work through the setbacks that will inevitably occur. What this looks like is the student working on an example—experiencing a setback or challenge—and being able to work through the challenge without being provided with assistance from the teacher.

What happens so often in classrooms, especially with students who struggle, is that learners begin to work through a problem or task and at the slightest experience of difficulty raise their hand and ask for the teacher's help. Rather than learn to persevere in the face of challenge, they are learning that each time they hit a roadblock, the teacher will remove it for them. If this occurs each time a challenge presents itself, they will quickly learn that someone else will help them overcome the obstacles (Guay et al., 2008; Reeve et al., 2008). How, then, can they learn to overcome them by themselves? Students will feel a knot in their stomach when they hit a roadblock—a difficult problem. But if they have already been shown the steps or how to solve the problem, and sufficient examples have been modeled and practiced, they will need to work through the setbacks on their own. The knot in their stomach will eventually dissipate as they work through the challenge and discover that they have the tools to solve it on their own. This is an essential feature of perseverance but one that many students don't have the opportunity to experience.

Reinforce All Efforts Toward Grit and Perseverance

The third and final condition necessary for the growth and development of perseverance is the ongoing reinforcement when students attempt gritty or stick-withitness behaviors, such as not giving up in the face of challenge. It is valuable to reinforce students when they persevere, such as when watching them work through a difficult mathematics problem autonomously. There are many synonyms for grit, and you can use these synonyms when reinforcing students. For example, you can say, "I like your moxie," "I really appreciate your persistence," or "I really like the way you are staying the course." What you reinforce is very likely to endure, and therefore students need you to reinforce their determination. On the topic of perseverance, Carol Dweck's research on fixed and growth mindset (2006, 2007, 2015; Yeager & Dweck, 2012) is a precursor to the conditions necessary to develop this disposition in our students.

Design Tasks to Elicit Flow

Getting back to perseverance, Mihaly Csikszentmihalyi's (2000, 2014) concept of flow is closely related. As mentioned earlier in this book, Csikszentmihalyi, the Hungarian-born psychologist, referred to *flow* as a highly focused mental state. His influential work titled *Flow: The Psychology of Optimal Experience* addresses the positive aspects of human experience (Csikszentmihalyi, 1990), termed as such because it emphasizes the concept of happiness, a concept that has eluded societies for years and is explained by Csikszentmihalyi as the control that one has over his or her situation.

One achieves this state of flow or supreme contentment when the work produces neither boredom nor anxiety (Csikszentmihalyi, 2000). Therefore, in order for students to be "in the flow," the work needs to have a focus or direction—a goal—and the individual must have the necessary skills to master the goal.

When this occurs, the individual is in the flow. The individual has lost all sense of space and time, forgets that he or she is sitting in a classroom and that it is 10:00 a.m. When a student is content with the work in which he or she is engaged, he or she is very likely to persevere (Gregory & Kaufeldt, 2015; Laursen, 2015). Therefore, the structure of the environment must be such that individuals want to persevere, often without even realizing it, because they are so immersed in the task at hand that they lose sight of the fact that they are in school and have been given a task to complete.

Unfortunately, students are sometimes presented with a task that is either beyond their capacity or too easy, thus leading to boredom. As Lev Vygotsky (1978) describes it, the task presented to the students is beyond their ZPD. Consequentially, if we want students to persevere, the task must be neither too easy nor too challenging, and a clear goal must be present.

Furthermore, flow leads to continued determination and improvement, and therefore the assigned task must continue to match the students' current level (Basawapatna, Repenning, Koh, & Nickerson 2013; Csikszentmihalyi, 2000; Vygotsky, 1978). Tiered learning, 2-5-8, choice boards, and other examples presented in chapter 6 (page 109) are highly effective in providing students with the appropriate level of challenge, enabling each student to experience the sensation of flow.

Value Quality Over Quantity

It would be helpful if schools reinforce the importance of quality over quantity. We have to reorganize the way we think about what learning and learning outcomes really are by sending the message to students that working on a task in earnest is valued, even if it means that the task in its entirety was not completed. For example, if a student is struggling through a mathematics problem, we can either reinforce his or her perseverance or inform the student that if he or she spends too much time on one problem, he or she won't be able to complete the worksheet. The former comment is far more likely to communicate the value of quality of work rather than quantity of examples completed, even if they are not done correctly. When students are sent the message that they need to work quickly and get it all done rather than work diligently, work methodically, and overcome challenges, they learn to value speed rather than developing grit.

The reproducible "Essential Elements of Grit and Perseverance" found on page 163 summarizes the strategies representing the essential elements of grit and perseverance.

◢ NEXT STEPS

There are four strategies you can try right away to enhance student grittiness. First, when students are visibly struggling with a skill, make sure that you have taught them the steps needed to be successful. Being successful doesn't mean completing the mathematics problem or responding to all the questions at the end of the chapter. It means getting into the game—having stamina. Therefore, teach the steps involved (in a mathematics problem, first you find the bracket and solve whatever is in the bracket, then you find the exponent . . .). Give students a checklist and have them mark off when each step in the process has been completed. If the steps are very explicit, they should be able to complete the problem independently, or at least some of the steps.

Second, when a student raises a hand asking for help, have the student wait a few minutes before you respond. Increase the amount of time you wait each day by a few minutes. Try to make sure that the student is using a checklist and moving from one step to the next.

Third, reinforce your students for their stamina and endurance. Hear yourself say, "You were able to work independently for fifteen minutes today. It's more important to keep on going than to get it right. Of course, you should adjust as needed, but the goal here is to keep on trying."

Finally, provide students with options for how they will show you what they've been learning. Tic-tac-toe boards, described in chapter 6 (page 141), are a great tool to use for this.

Write down each time you try any one of these four strategies. Write down what you did as well as a reflection. How did it feel? How did your student respond?

Essential Elements of Grit and Perseverance

ELEMENT	EXAMPLE
Teaching necessary skills and procedures	Teach students the skills and procedures that they need in order to master the task. This almost always involves teaching them a series of steps. For example, PALS (specifically shrink-the-paragraph) is an evidence-based strategy, one part of which involves teaching students how to hold onto the subject of each sentence.
Teaching autonomy	Once the strategies have been presented and the steps have been taught, it's important to allow students to struggle through the practice of the skill toward developing automaticity. Students will call on you to help them. Try to resist the urge to do it for them, but rather give them the confidence and the direction to move through the steps, one at a time, each day working autonomously a little bit longer than the day before.
Reinforcing all efforts	Reinforce all approximations toward developing grit and perseverance. We tend to engage in behaviors that are reinforced and stay away from behaviors that are not reinforced or ignored. When students show efforts toward following that checklist when completing a mathematics problem rather than raising their hand to ask for help, they should be reinforced with a comment such as "I really like the way you persevered and continued to work on the problem even when one of the steps was somewhat difficult for you."

Flow	Provide students with work that is at or just above their readiness level, rather than work that is overly challenging. Additionally, as often as possible, allow students to work on material or content that is of interest to them. You can allow them to choose a fiction or nonfiction text that relates to an area of interest, or allow them to go into greater depth in a particular aspect of the curriculum. For example, they could study their animal of choice or examine a time period in history that they find most intriguing.
Quality over quantity	Reinforce to students that it is better to work through one example than quickly, yet incorrectly, work through all problems on a worksheet. If you reinforce the student for persevering though a problem with comments such as "I really appreciate your persistence with that problem," you will likely see more of this type of behavior. When we reinforce quality with comments such as "You've only completed two examples, so you'd better hurry up as you won't have time to complete all of your work," we will likely encourage quantity over quality of work.

Strategies to Teach Students How to Persevere

STRATEGY	EXAMPLE *What did you do?*	REFLECTION *How do you think it worked? How did your students respond?*
Teach students steps and provide students with a checklist.		
Autonomy: Wait a few minutes more each day before providing help to students. Have them work through the steps using their checklist.		
Reinforce their stamina and endurance.		
Use a tic-tac-toe board.		

EPILOGUE

We Are the Changemakers

Ultimately, the message that I aspired to communicate in this book is that the most effective teachers are mindful and purposeful and it's up to us to catch ourselves when we are being mindless or feeling dispassionate, when we get stale or uncreative in our jobs.

The goal for both the parent and the teacher is to transition an infant or young child, who is initially completely dependent, to an adolescent and ultimately an adult who is independent, capable, and confident. With our words, but more important with our actions, students are learning to be accepting of others, to welcome difference or not, and to be part of an ecosystem whereby all are valued for their contributions as well as their weaknesses. We as teachers are responsible in large part for orchestrating that environment. When we accept the variability, the messiness in teaching, and the factors that influence the outcomes, we can come to appreciate the diversity that exists in all classrooms. In the words of Sizer and Sizer (2000), "The students are watching."

Equally important—to use the architecture analogy (Hitchcock et al., 2002; Stanford & Reeves, 2009)—is to build supporting walls and a solid foundation, or the house will fall down. The tensions that educators face on a daily basis relate to the questions, How tight or loose do I wish to be as an educator? Do I follow a series of principles, guidelines, and target goals, or do I focus on creating an environment that is nourishing but not overly scripted and planned so that students will become resilient and independent thinkers?

As with any other profession, there are fundamentals to teaching that you must apply first. Once these fundamentals are present, build a unique and distinctive home. Make it as creative and quirky as you like—make sure it represents your personality—but remember that this will only be possible if the fundamentals are there. I'm all for professional autonomy, provided it doesn't impinge on excellence. Progress is a result of reflective, mindful, and purposeful practice (Tomlinson, 1999, 2001, 2014)—"I did this and it didn't work, so I'm going to try something different." Teach your students purposefully, methodically, and slowly. Give extra time to those who need it; get evidence—and then do something with the evidence! That is how you identify progress. I say to teachers all the time, "Absolutely, be as creative as you want, but where there is solid evidence that these teaching fundamentals increase success, why not use them?"

According to a plethora of research that has been gathered in many instances in the format of a meta-analysis or synthesis of many research articles, there are very specific strategies that, when employed by teachers, help students do better (Brush & Saye, 2000; Chappuis & Stiggins, 2002; Dunlosky et al., 2013; Dweck, 2006; Gordon, 2001; Marzano, 2009b; Marzano & Brown, 2009; Marzano & Marzano, 2001). To name a few examples highlighted in this book, the articulation and communication of target goals and the ongoing evaluation of student mastery have been shown to improve student learning (Bates, 2015; Cleary et al., 2017; Jansen et al., 2009; Tomlinson, 1999, 2001; Wiggins & McTighe, 1998). Put simply, when teachers use these strategies, students do better.

Years ago, people were dying from the slightest infections (Jones, Podolsky, & Greene, 2012). When antibiotics were invented, in many cases infections became no more serious than the common cold, if treated immediately. In education, like in medicine and other professions, when teachers employ specific strategies, what could have been a long-lasting and serious impediment can now be addressed, enabling most students to thrive. The research is there—let's use it. Of course, all teachers should themselves do research, examine the results, use the data, and make adjustments as needed. There is nothing more satisfying than the look of I-get-it-and-I-can-do-this on students' faces when what they learned made perfect sense. And then, they are able to put it into practice and the shift happens. Therein lies the ultimate golden nugget of meaning and purpose of what we can bring to education. This is the way through to effective teaching and learning. This is what it means to be both mindful and purposeful, and it is how you can leave lasting impact.

The role of the teacher is to provide gifts to students in the way of strategic learning approaches that will remain with the students for a lifetime. Assume the role of both carpenter *and* gardener by incorporating best practices and creating ecosystems that nourish student growth and independence—and most of all, welcome variability and diversity.

REFERENCES AND RESOURCES

24/7 Sports. (n.d.). *Vince Lombardi quotes: #8.* Accessed at https://247sports
.com/Coach/3614/Quotes/Practice-does-not-make-perfect-Only-
perfect-practice
-makes-perfe-35987400 on April 24, 2020.

Achinstein, B., & Barrett, A. (2004). (Re)framing classroom contexts: How
new teachers and mentors view diverse learners and challenges of
practice. *Teachers College Record, 106*(4), 716–746.

Alamri, H., Lowell, V., Watson, W., & Watson, S. L. (2020). Using
personalized learning as an instructional approach to motivate
learners in online higher education: Learner self-determination
and intrinsic motivation. *Journal of Research on Technology in
Education, 52*(3), 322–352.

Allen, D., & Tanner, K. (2006). Rubrics: Tools for making learning goals
and evaluation criteria explicit for both teachers and learners. *CBE -
Life Sciences Education, 5*(3), 197–295.

Alter, P., & Haydon, T. (2017). Characteristics of effective classroom
rules: A review of the literature. *Teacher Education and Special
Education, 40*(2), 114–127.

Ames, C. (1990). Motivation: What teachers need to know. *Teachers College
Record, 91*(3), 409–421.

Ames, C. A. (1992). Classrooms: Goals, structures, and student motivation.
Journal of Educational Psychology, 84, 261–271.

Anderson, L. W., Krathwohl, D. R., Airasian, P. W., Cruikshank, K. A.,
Mayer, R. E., Pintrich, P. R., et al. (2001). *A taxonomy for learning,
teaching, and assessing: A revision of Bloom's taxonomy of educational
objectives* (Abridged ed.). White Plains, NY: Longman.

Anderson-Inman, L., Walker, H. M., & Purcell, J. (1984). Promoting the transfer of skills across settings: Transenvironmental programming for handicapped students in the mainstream. In W. L. Heward, T. E. Heron, D. S. Hill, & J. Trap-Porter (Eds.), *Focus on behavior analysis in education* (pp. 18–37). Columbus, OH: Merrill.

Angelo, T. A., & Patricia-Cross, K. (1993). *Classroom assessment techniques: A handbook for college teachers* (2nd ed.). San Francisco, CA: Jossey-Bass.

Archer, A. L., & Hughes, C. A. (2010). Exploring the foundations of explicit teaching. In *Explicit instruction: Effective and efficient teaching* (pp. 1–21). New York, NY: Guilford Press.

Arends, R. (1991). *Learning to teach* (2nd ed.). New York, NY: McGraw-Hill.

Ayers, W., Klonsky, M., & Lyon, G. H. (Eds.). (2000). *A simple justice: The challenge of small schools.* New York, NY: Teachers College Press.

Ayllon, T., & Michael, J. (1959). The psychiatric nurse as a behavioral engineer. *Journal of the Experimental Analysis of Behavior, 2*(4), 323–334.

Bachhel, R., & Thaman, R. G. (2014). Effective use of pause procedure to enhance student engagement and learning. *Journal of Clinical & Diagnostic Research, 8*(8), 1–3.

Baker, P. H. (2005). Managing student behavior: How ready are teachers to meet the challenge? *American Secondary Education, 33*(3), 51–64.

Ball, D. L., & Cohen, D. K. (1996). Reform by the book: What is—or might be—the role of curriculum materials in teacher learning and instructional reform? *Educational Researcher, 25*(9), 6–14.

Bandura, A. (1986). *Social foundations of thought and action: A social cognitive theory.* Englewood Cliffs, NJ: Prentice Hall.

Barbetta, P. M., Norona, K. L., & Bicard, D. F. (2005). Classroom behavior management: A dozen common mistakes and what to do instead. *Preventing School Failure: Alternative Education for Children and Youth, 49*(3), 11–19.

Baron, J. (2000). *Thinking and deciding* (3rd ed.). New York, NY: Cambridge University Press.

Basawapatna, A. R., Repenning, A., Koh, K. H., & Nickerson, H. (2013, August). *The zones of proximal flow: Guiding students through a space of computational thinking skills and challenges.* The Ninth Annual International ACM Conference on International Computing. Paper presented in California, USA.

Bates, A. W. (2015). *Teaching in a digital age: Guidelines for designing teaching and learning.* Vancouver, BC, Canada: Tony Bates Associates.

Beecher, M., & Sweeny, S. M. (2008). Closing the achievement gap with curriculum enrichment and differentiation: One school's story. *Journal of Advanced Academics, 19*(3), 502–530.

Berry, R. A. W. (2008). Novice teachers' conceptions of fairness in inclusion classrooms. *Teaching and Teacher Education, 24*(5), 1149–1159.

Berry, R. A. W. (2010). Preservice and early career teachers' attitudes toward inclusion, instructional accommodations, and fairness: Three profiles. *The Teacher Educator, 45*(2), 75–95.

Biggs, J. (1996). Enhancing teaching through constructive alignment. *Higher Education, 32,* 347–364.

Biggs, J. (1999). What the student does: Teaching for enhanced learning. *Higher Education Research and Development, 18*(1), 57–75.

Binet, A., & Simon, T. (1961). The development of intelligence in children. In J. J. Jenkins & D. G. Paterson (Eds.), *Studies in individual differences: The search for intelligence* (pp. 81–111). East Norwalk, CT: Appleton-Century-Crofts.

Black, P., Harrison, C., Lee, C., Marshall, B., & Wiliam, D. (2004). Working inside the black box: Assessment for learning in the classroom. *Phi Delta Kappan, 86*(1), 8–21.

Black, P. J., & Wiliam, D. (1998a). Assessment and classroom learning. *Assessment in Education: Principles, Policy and Practice, 5*(1), 7–74.

Black, P., & Wiliam, D. (1998b). Inside the black box. *Phi Delta Kappan, 80*(2), 139–148.

Black, P., & Wiliam, D. (2005). *Inside the black box: Raising standards through classroom assessment.* Brentford, UK: Granada Learning.

Black, P., & Wiliam, D. (2009). Developing the theory of formative assessment. *Educational Assessment, Evaluation and Accountability, 21*(1), 5–31.

Black, P., & Wiliam, D. (2012). Developing a theory of formative assessment. In J. Gardner (Ed.), *Assessment and learning.* New York, NY: SAGE.

Blackwell, L. S., Rodriguez, S., & Guerra-Carrillo, B. (2014). Intelligence as a malleable construct. In S. Goldstein, D. Princiotta, & J. A. Naglieri (Eds.), *Handbook of intelligence: Evolutionary theory, historical perspective, and current concepts.* New York, NY: Springer.

Bloom, B. S., Englehart, M. D., Furst, E. J., Hill, W. H., & Krathwohl, D. R. (1956). *Taxonomy of educational objectives handbook 1: The cognitive domain.* New York, NY: David McKay.

Brame, C., & Director, C. A. (2018). *Just-in-time teaching (JiTT).* Center for Teaching, Vanderbilt University. Accessed at http://cft.vanderbilt.edu/guides-sub-pages/just -in-timeteaching-jitt on July 14, 2020.

Brand, S. T., & Dalton, E. M. (2012). Universal design for learning: Cognitive theory into practice for facilitating comprehension in early literacy. *Forum on Public Policy Online, 2012*(1), 1–19.

Brennan, A. (2019). Differentiation through choice as an approach to enhance inclusive practice. *Reach, 32*(1), 11–20.

Brooks, C. F., & Young, S. L. (2011). Are choice-making opportunities needed in the classroom? Using self-determination theory to consider student motivation and learner empowerment. *International Journal of Teaching and Learning in Higher Education, 23*(1), 48–59.

Brophy, J. (1986). Classroom management techniques. *Education and Urban Society, 18*(2), 182–194.

Brophy, J., & Good, T. (1986). Teacher behavior and student achievement. In M. C. Wittrock (Ed.), *Handbook of research on teaching* (3rd ed., pp. 375–391). New York, NY: Macmillan.

Brown, A. L., & Palincsar, A. S. (1987). *Reciprocal teaching of comprehension strategies: A natural history of one program for enhancing learning.* New York, NY: Ablex.

Brundage, E. (1953). Teaching the individual adolescent. *Educational Leadership, 11*(3), 147–151.

Brush, T., & Saye, J. (2000). Implementation and evaluation of a student-centered learning unit: A case study. *Educational Technology Research and Development, 48*(3), 79–100.

Bucholz, J. E., & Sheffler, J. L. (2009). Creating a warm and inclusive classroom environment: Planning for all children to feel welcome. *Electronic Journal for Inclusive Education, 2*(4), 1–13.

Byrnes, J. P. (1996). *Cognitive development and learning in instructional contexts.* Boston, MA: Allyn and Bacon.

Caine, R. N., & Caine, G. (1991). *Making connections teaching and the human brain.* Alexandria, VA: Association for Supervision and Curriculum Development.

Cameron, J., & Pierce, W. D. (1994). Reinforcement, reward, and intrinsic motivation: A meta-analysis. *Review of Educational Research, 64*(3), 363–423.

CAST. (2011). *Universal design for learning guidelines version 2.0.* Wakefield, MA: Author.

Chaiklin, S. (2003). The zone of proximal development in Vygotsky's analysis of learning and instruction. In A. Kozulin, B. Grindis, V. S. Ageyev, & S. M. Miller (Eds.), *Learning in doing: Vygotsky's educational theory in cultural context,* (Vol. 1, pp. 39–64). Cambridge, UK: Cambridge University Press.

Chapman, C., & King, R. (2011). *Differentiated assessment strategies: One tool doesn't fit all.* Thousand Oaks, CA: Corwin.

Chappuis, S., & Stiggins, R. J. (2002). Classroom assessment for learning. *Educational Leadership, 60*(1), 40–43.

Chard, D. J., Vaughn, S., & Tyler, B. J. (2002). A synthesis of research on effective interventions for building reading fluency with elementary students with learning disabilities. *Journal of Learning Disabilities, 35*(5), 386–406.

Cheeseman, J., Clarke, D., Roche, A., & Walker, N. (2016). Introducing challenging tasks: Inviting and clarifying without explaining and demonstrating. *Australian Primary Mathematics Classroom, 21*(3), 3.

Chesebro, J. L., & McCroskey, J. C. (2001). The relationship of teacher clarity and immediacy with student state receiver apprehension, affect and cognitive learning. *Communication Education, 50*(1), 59–68.

Childe, A., Sands, J. P., & Pope, S. T. (2009). Backward design. *Teaching Exceptional Children, 41*(5), 6–14.

Chitiyo, M., & Wheeler, J. J. (2009). Challenges faced by school teachers in implementing positive behavior support in their school systems. *Remedial and Special Education, 30*(1), 58–63.

Choy, S. C., & Cheah, P. K. (2009). Teacher perceptions of critical thinking among students and its influence on higher education. *International Journal of Teaching and Learning in Higher Education, 20*(2), 198–206.

Cleary, J., Morgan, T., & Marzano, R. J. (2017). *Classroom techniques for creating conditions for rigorous instruction*. West Palm Beach, FL: Learning Sciences International.

Collins, A., Brown, J. S., & Holum, A. (1991). Cognitive apprenticeship: Making thinking visible. *American Educator, 15*(3), 6–11.

Collins, A., Brown, J. S., & Newman, S. E. (1989). Cognitive apprenticeship: Teaching the crafts of reading, writing, and mathematics. In L. B. Resnick (Ed.), *Knowing, learning, and instruction: Essays in honor of Robert Glaser* (pp. 453–494). Hillside, NJ: Lawrence Erlbaum Associates.

Cone, J. D. (1997). Issues on functional analysis in behavioral assessment. *Behavior Research and Therapy, 35*(3), 259–275.

Connolly, P. (2009). The challenges and prospects for educational effectiveness research. *Effective Education, 1*(1), 1–12.

Conroy, M. A., & Sutherland, K. S. (2012). Effective teachers for students with emotional /behavioral disorders: Active ingredients leading to positive teacher and student outcomes. *Beyond Behavior, 22*(1), 7–13.

Coon, D. (2001). *Introduction to psychology: Gateways to mind and behavior* (9th ed.). London UK: Wadsworth.

Cordova, D. I., & Lepper, M. R. (1996). Intrinsic motivation and the process of learning: Beneficial effects of contextualization, personalization, and choice. *Journal of Educational Psychology, 88*(4), 715–730.

Covey, S. (1989). *The 7 habits of highly effective people.* New York, NY: Free Press.

Csikszentmihalyi, M. (1990). Flow: The psychology of optimal experience. *Journal of Leisure Research, 24*(1), 93–94.

Csikszentmihalyi, M. (2000). *Beyond boredom and anxiety.* San Francisco, CA: Jossey-Bass.

Csikszentmihalyi, M. (2014). Toward a psychology of optimal experience. In M. Csikszentmihalyi (Ed.), *Flow and the foundations of positive psychology: The collected works of Mihaly Csikszentmihalyi* (Vol. 3, pp. 209–226). Dordrecht, Netherlands: Springer.

Csikszentmihalyi, M., & Csikszentmihalyi, I. S. (1992). *Optimal experience: Psychological studies of flow in consciousness.* Cambridge, UK: Cambridge University Press.

Darling-Hammond, L. (2007). Teacher learning that supports student learning. In B. Z. Presseisen (Ed.), *Teaching for intelligence* (2nd ed.). Thousand Oaks, CA: Corwin.

Darling-Hammond, L., & Snyder, J. (2000). Authentic assessment of teaching in context. *Teaching and Teacher Education, 16*(5–6), 523–545.

Dean, C. B., Hubbell, E. R., Pitler, H., & Stone, B. (2012). *Classroom instruction that works.* Alexandria, VA: Association for Supervision and Curriculum Development.

Deci, E. L. (1971). Effects of externally mediated rewards on intrinsic motivation. *Journal of Personality and Social Psychology, 18*, 105–115.

Deci, E. L., Eghrari, H., Patrick, B. C., & Leone, D. R. (1994). Facilitating internalization: The self-determination theory perspective. *Journal of Personality, 62*(1), 119–142.

Deci, E. L., & Ryan, R. M. (2002). Overview of self-determination theory: An organismic dialectical perspective. In E. L. Deci & R. M. Ryan (Eds.), *Handbook of self-determination research.* New York, NY: University of Rochester Press.

Deci, E. L., & Ryan, R. M. (2010). Intrinsic motivation. *The Corsini Encyclopedia of Psychology,* pp. 1–2.

Deci, E. L., & Ryan, R. M. (2011). Self-determination theory. In P. A. M. Van Lange, A. W. Kruglanski, & E. T. Higgins (Eds.), *Handbook of theories of social psychology: collection: Volumes 1 & 2.* Thousand Oaks, CA: SAGE.

De Jong, T. (2010). Cognitive load theory, educational research, and instructional design: Some food for thought. *Instructional Science, 38*(2), 105–134.

Dennen, V. P., & Burner, K. J. (2008). The cognitive apprenticeship model in educational practice. In D. Jonassen, M. J. Spector, M. Driscoll, M. D. Merrill, J. Van Merrienboer, & M. P. Driscoll (Eds.), *Handbook of research on educational communications and technology* (pp. 425–439). New York, NY: Routledge.

Dewey, J. (1993). *The political writings.* Indianapolis, IN: Hackett.

Dixson, D. D., & Worrell, F. C. (2016). Formative and summative assessment in the classroom. *Theory Into Practice, 55*(2), 153–159.

Donovan, M. S., & Bransford, J. D. (2005). *How students learn.* Washington, DC: National Academies Press.

Doolittle, P. E. (1997). Vygotsky's zone of proximal development as a theoretical foundation for cooperative learning. *Journal on Excellence in College Teaching, 8*(1), 83–103.

Dotger, S., & Causton-Theoharis, J. (2010). Differentiation through choice: Using a think-tac-toe for science content. *Science Scope, 33*(6), 18–23.

Dreyfus, S. E., & Dreyfus, H. L. (1980). *A five-stage model of the mental activities involved in directed skill acquisition.* Berkeley: California University Berkeley Operations Research Center.

Drill, K., Miller, S., & Behrstock-Sherratt, E. (2012). Teachers' perspectives on educational research. *American Institute for Research: Education, human development, and the workforce.* Accessed at https://files.eric.ed.gov/fulltext/ED530742.pdf on April 28, 2020.

Duckworth, A. L., Peterson, C., Matthews, M. D., & Kelly, D. R. (2007). Grit: perseverance, and passion for long-term goals. *Journal of Personality and Social Psychology, 92*(6), 1087–1101.

Duckworth, A. (2016). *Grit: The power of passion and perseverance.* New York, NY: Simon & Schuster.

Duckworth, A. L., Quinn, P. D., Lynam, D. R., Loeber, R., & Stouthamer-Loeber, M. (2011). Role of test motivation in intelligence testing. *Proceedings of the National Academy of Sciences, 108*(19), 7716–7720.

Duckworth, K., Akerman, R., MacGregor, A., Salter, E., & Vorhaus, J. (2009). Self-regulated learning: A literature review [Wider Benefits of Learning Research Report No. 33]. *Centre for Research on the Wider Benefits of Learning.* Accessed at http://discovery.ucl.ac.uk/1520492/1/WBLResRep33.pdf on April 28, 2020.

Dunbar, C. (2004). *Best practices in classroom management.* Accessed at https://msu.edu/~dunbarc/dunbar3.pdf on April 28, 2020.

Dunlosky, J., Rawson, K. A., Marsh, E. J., Nathan, M. J., & Willingham, D. T. (2013). Improving students' learning with effective learning techniques: Promising directions from cognitive and educational psychology. *Psychological Science in the Public Interest, 14*(1), 4–58.

Durand, V. M. (1987). "Look homeward angel": A call to return to our (functional) roots. *Behavior Analyst, 10*, 299–302.

Dweck, C. S. (2006). *Mindset: The new psychology of success.* New York, NY: Random House.

Dweck, C. S. (2007). The perils and promises of praise. *Educational Leadership, 65*(2), 34–39.

Dweck, C. S. (2010). Even geniuses work hard. *Educational Leadership, 68*(1), 16–20.

Dweck, C. S. (2014a). Teachers' mindsets: "Every student has something to teach me": Feeling overwhelmed? Where did your natural teaching talent go? Try pairing a growth mindset with reasonable goals, patience, and reflection instead. It's time to get gritty and be a better teacher. *Educational Horizons, 93*(2), 10–15.

Dweck, C. S. (2014b). Mindsets and math/science achievement. *The opportunity equation: Transforming mathematics and science education for citizenship and the global economy* [Prepared for the Carnegie Corporation of New York Institute for Advanced Study Commission on Mathematics and Science Education]. Accessed at http://www .growthmindsetmaths.com/uploads/2/3/7/7/23776169/mindset_and_math_science _achievement_-_nov_2013.pdf on April 28, 2020.

Dweck, C. (2015). Carol Dweck revisits the growth mindset. *Education Week, 35*(5), 20–24.

Dye, G. A. (2000). Graphic organizers to the rescue! Helping students link—and remember—information. *Teaching Exceptional Children, 32*(3), 72–76.

Earl, L. M. (2012). *Assessment as learning: Using classroom assessment to maximize student learning* (2nd ed.). Thousand Oaks, CA: Corwin.

Entwistle, A., & Entwistle, N. (1992). Experiences of understanding in revising for degree examinations. *Learning and Instruction, 2*(1), 1–22.

Erickson, F. (1996a). Going for the zone: The social and cognitive ecology of teacher-student interaction in classroom conversations. *Discourse, Learning, and Schooling, pp.* 29–62.

Erickson, F. (1996b). Inclusion into what? Thoughts on the construction of learning, identity, and affiliation in the general education classroom. In D. L. Speece & B. K. Keogh (Eds.), *Research on classroom ecologies: Implications for inclusion of children with learning disabilities* (pp. 91–106). New York, NY: Routledge.

Evertson, C. M. (1994). *Classroom management for elementary teachers.* Boston, MA: Allyn & Bacon.

Fancourt, A., & Holmes, J. (2020). Impact of working memory and learning difficulties in the classroom. In J. Harrington, J. Beale, A. Fancourt, & C. Lutz (Eds.), *The "BrainCanDo" handbook of teaching and learning: Practical strategies to bring psychology and neuroscience into the classroom.* London, UK: Routledge.

Feuerstein, R., Feuerstein, R., & Falik, L. H. (2015). *Beyond smarter: Mediated learning and the brain's capacity for change.* New York, NY: Teachers College Press.

Feuerstein, R., & Jensen, M. R. (1980). Instrumental enrichment: Theoretical basis, goals, and instruments. *The Educational Forum, 44*(4), 401–423.

Feuerstein, R., Klein, P. S., & Tannenbaum, A. J. (1991). *Mediated learning experience (MLE): Theoretical, psychosocial and learning implications.* Tel Aviv, Israel: Freund Publishing House.

Feuerstein, R., Miller, R., Hoffman, M. B., Rand, Y. A., Mintzker, Y., & Jensen, M. R. (1981). Cognitive modifiability in adolescence: Cognitive structure and the effects of intervention. *The Journal of Special Education, 15*(2), 269–287.

Feuerstein, R., Rand, Y. A., Hoffman, M., Hoffman, M., & Miller, R. (1979). Cognitive modifiability in retarded adolescents: Effects of instrumental enrichment. *American Journal of Mental Deficiency, 83*(6), 539–550.

Fisher, D., & Frey, N. (2008). *Better learning through structured teaching: A framework for the gradual release of responsibility.* Alexandria, VA: Association for Supervision and Curriculum Development.

Fisher, D., & Frey, N. (2019). Show and tell: A video column / A map for meaningful learning. *Educational Leadership, 75*(5), 82–83.

Fisher, D., Frey, N., & Hattie, J. (2016). *Visible learning for literacy, grades K–12: Implementing the practices that work best to accelerate student learning.* Thousand Oaks, CA: Corwin.

Frederickson, N., & Turner, J. (2003). Utilizing the classroom peer group to address children's social needs: An evaluation of the circle of friends intervention approach. *The Journal of Special Education, 36*(4), 234–245. doi:10.1177/002246690303600404

Freire, P. (1970). *Pedagogy of the oppressed.* New York, NY: Herder & Herder.

Frey, N., Hattie, J., & Fisher, D. (2018). Understand where they are going and have confidence to take on the challenge. In *Developing assessment-capable visible learners, grades K–12: Maximizing skill, will, and thrill* (pp. 37–53). Thousand Oaks, CA: Corwin.

Fuchs, D., & Fuchs, L. S. (1994). Inclusive schools movement and the radicalization of special education reform. *Exceptional Children, 60*(4), 294–309.

Fuchs, D., Fuchs, L. S., & Burish, P. (2000). Peer-assisted learning strategies: An evidence-based practice to promote reading achievement. *Learning Disabilities Research and Practice, 15*(2), 85–91.

Fullan, M. (1994). Coordinating top-down and bottom-up strategies for educational reform. In R. J. Anson (Ed.), *Systemic reform: Perspectives on personalizing education* (pp. 7–24). Washington, DC: U.S. Department of Education.

Furrer, C. J., Skinner, E. A., & Pitzer, J. R. (2014). The influence of teacher and peer relationships on students' classroom engagement and everyday motivational resilience. *National Society for the Study of Education, 113*(1), 101–123.

Gage, N. A., Lewis, T. J., & Stichter, J. P. (2012). Functional behavioral assessment-based interventions for students with or at risk for emotional and/or behavioral disorders in school: A hierarchical linear modeling meta-analysis. *Behavioral Disorders, 37*(2), 55–77. doi:10.1177/019874291203700201

Gardner, H. (1983). *Frames of mind: The theory of multiple intelligences.* New York, NY: Basic Books.

Giallo, R., & Little, E. (2003). Classroom behaviour problems: The relationship between preparedness, classroom experiences, and self-efficacy in graduate and student teachers. *Australian Journal of Educational and Developmental Psychology, 3*(1), 21–34.

Gleason, M. M., Goldson, E., Yogman, M. W., & Council on Early Childhood. (2016). Addressing early childhood emotional and behavioral problems. *Pediatrics, 138*(6). Accessed at https://www.researchgate.net/profile/Mary_Margaret_Gleason /publication/310665646_Addressing_Early_Childhood_Emotional_and _Behavioral_Problems/links/5acec71baca2723a33443c65/Addressing-Early -Childhood-Emotional-and-Behavioral-Problems.pdf on July 14, 2020.

Gonzalez, G., & Leticia, M. (2013). Learning goals and strategies in the self-regulation of learning. *US-China Education Review, 3*(1), 46–50.

Gopnik, A. (2016). *The gardener and the carpenter.* New York, NY: Farrar, Straus & Giroux.

Gordon, L. M. (2001). *Higher teacher efficacy as a marker of teacher effectiveness in the domain of classroom management.* Paper presented at the annual meeting of the California Council on Teacher Education, October 25–27, San Diego, CA.

Goswami, U. (2008). Principles of learning, implications for teaching: A cognitive neuroscience perspective. *Journal of Philosophy of Education, 42*(3–4), 381–399.

Graham, S., & Perin, D. (2007). *Writing next: Effective strategies to improve writing of adolescents in middle and high schools.* Washington, DC: Alliance for Excellent Education.

Green, J. M. (1998, February). *Constructing the way forward for all students.* A speech delivered at the "Innovations for Effective Schools" OECD/New Zealand joint follow-up conference, Christchurch, New Zealand.

Gregory, G. H., & Chapman, C. (2012). *Differentiated instructional strategies: One size doesn't fit all* (3rd ed.). Thousand Oaks, CA: Corwin.

Gregory, G., & Kaufeldt, M. (2015). *The motivated brain: Improving student attention, engagement, and perseverance.* Alexandria, VA: Association for Supervision and Curriculum Development.

Grisham-Brown, J., Hallam, R., & Brookshire, R. (2006). Using authentic assessment to evidence children's progress toward early learning standards. *Early Childhood Education Journal, 34*(1), 45–51.

Grubaugh, S., & Houston, R. (1990). Establishing a classroom environment that promotes interaction and improved student behavior. *The Clearing House, 63*(8), 375–378.

Guay, F., Ratelle, C. F., & Chanal, J. (2008). Optimal learning in optimal contexts: The role of self-determination in education. *Canadian Psychology, 49*(3), 233–240.

Guskey, T. R. (2010). Lessons of mastery learning. *Educational Leadership, 68*(2), 52–57.

Guthrow, J. (2002). *Correlation between high rates of corporal punishment in public schools and pathologies.* Accessed at http://www.nospank.net /correlationstudy.htm on April 27, 2020.

Hagborg, W. J. (1992). Grades and motivational orientation among high school students. *Journal of Psychoeducational Assessment, 10*(4), 355–361. doi:10.1177/073428299201000405

Hall, T. (2002). *Differentiated instruction.* Wakefield, MA: National Center on Accessing the General Curriculum.

Hart, S., Dixon, A., Drummond, M. J., & McIntyre, D. (2004). *Learning without limits.* Maidenhead, UK: Open University Press.

Hattie, J. (2003). *Teachers make a difference, what is the research evidence?* Paper presented at the Building Teacher Quality: What Does the Research Tell Us ACER Research Conference, Melbourne, Australia, October 19–21, 2003.

Hattie, J. (2008). *Visible learning: A synthesis of over 800 meta-analyses relating to achievement.* New York, NY: Routledge.

Hattie, J. (2012). *Visible learning for teachers: Maximizing impact on learning.* New York, NY: Routledge.

Hattie, J., Biggs, J., & Purdie, N. (1996). Effects of learning skills interventions on student learning: A meta-analysis. *Review of Educational Research, 66*(2), 99–136.

Hattie, J. A., & Donoghue, G. M. (2016). Learning strategies: A synthesis and conceptual model. *NPJ Science of Learning, 1*(16013), 1–13. doi.org/10.1038/npjscilearn.2016.13

Hattie, J., & Timperley, H. (2007). The power of feedback. *Review of Educational Research, 77*(1), 81–112.

Haycock, K. (1998). Good teaching matters: How well-qualified teachers can close the gap. *Thinking K–16, 3*(2), 1–19.

Haycock, K. (2017). Overview: Collaboration and student achievement: Educating for leadership and sustainability. In M. Mardis (Ed.), *Librarians and educators collaborating for success: The international perspective* (pp. 245–256). Santa Barbara, CA: ABC-CLIO.

Heacox, D. (2012). *Differentiating instruction in the regular classroom: How to reach and teach all learners.* Minneapolis, MN: Free Spirits.

Heritage, M. (2007). Formative assessment: What do teachers need to know and do? *Phi Delta Kappan, 89*(2), 140–145.

Heritage, M. (2010). *Formative assessment: Making it happen in the classroom.* Thousand Oaks, CA: Corwin.

Heritage, M. (2011). Formative assessment: An enabler of learning. Accessed at https://s3.amazonaws.com/amplify-assets/regional/Heritage_FA.pdf on April 27, 2020.

Hitchcock, C., Meyer, A., Rose, D., & Jackson, R. (2002). Providing new access to the general curriculum: Universal design for learning. *Teaching Exceptional Children, 35*(2), 8–17.

Hochanadel, A., & Finamore, D. (2015). Fixed and growth mindset in education and how grit helps students persist in the face of adversity. *Journal of International Education Research, 11*(1), 47–50.

Hockett, J. A., & Doubet, K. J. (2013). Turning on the lights: What pre-assessments can do. *Educational Leadership, 71*(4), 50–54.

Hodgson, P., & Pang, M. Y. (2012). Effective formative e-assessment of student learning: A study on a statistics course. *Assessment & Evaluation in Higher Education, 37*(2), 215–225.

Hoerr, T. R. (2013). *Fostering grit: How do I prepare my students for the real world?* Alexandria, VA: Association for Supervision and Curriculum Development.

Hogan, K., & Pressley, M. (1997). *Scaffolding scientific competencies within classroom communities of inquiry.* Cambridge, MA: Brookline Books.

Holley, L. C., & Steiner, S. (2005). Safe space: Student perspectives on classroom environment. *Journal of Social Work Education, 41*(1), 49–64.

Hughes, L. E., & Wilkins, A. J. (2002). Reading at a distance: Implications for the design of text in children's big books. *British Journal of Educational Psychology, 72*(2), 213–226.

Huitt, W. (2003). The information processing approach to cognition. *Educational Psychology Interactive, 3*(2), 53–67.

Hulac, D. M., & Briesch, A. M. (2017). *Evidence-based strategies for effective classroom management.* New York, NY: Guilford Press.

Hultberg, P., Calonge, D. S., & Lee, A. E. S. (2018). Promoting long-lasting learning through instructional design. *Journal of Scholarship of Teaching and Learning, 18*(3), 26–43.

Ilhan-Beyaztas, D., & Dawson, E. (2017). A cross-national study of student teachers' views about intelligence: Similarities and differences in England and Turkey. *Universal Journal of Educational Research, 5*(3), 510–516. doi:10.13189/ujer.2017.050324

International Consulting and Trade Associates, Inc. (n.d.). *FIE standard version: Improving cognitive ability*. Accessed at http://thinkingtolearn.org/program-description-for -standard/ on April 27, 2020.

International Renewal Institute. (n.d.). *Feuerstein's instrumental enrichment: Standard level program*. Accessed at www.faculty.umb.edu/peter_taylor/601/files/FIE%20 Standard%20Sample%20iRi%205-19-13%2C%20complete.pdf on November 2, 2020.

Israel, M., Maynard, K., & Williamson, P. (2013). Promoting literacy-embedded, authentic STEM instruction for students with disabilities and other struggling learners. *Teaching Exceptional Children, 45*(4), 18–25.

Iwata, B. A., Wallace, M. D., Kahng, S., Lindberg, J. S., Roscoe, E. M., Conners, J., et al. (2000). Skill acquisition in the implementation of functional analysis methodology. *Journal of Applied Behavior Analysis, 33*(2), 181–194. doi:10.1901/jaba.2000.33-181

Iyengar, S. S., & Lepper, M. R. (1999). Rethinking the value of choice: A cultural perspective on intrinsic motivation. *Journal of Personality and Social Psychology, 76*(3), 349–366.

James, G. (2016). Making sense of behaviour problems. In *Transforming behaviour in the classroom: A solution-focused guide for new teachers* (pp. 79–89). London, UK: SAGE.

Jansen, A., Bartell, T., & Berk, D. (2009). The role of learning goals in building a knowledge base for elementary mathematics teacher education. *The Elementary School Journal, 109*(5), 525–536. doi:10.1086/597000

Jennings, P. A., & Greenberg, M. T. (2009). The prosocial classroom: Teacher social and emotional competence in relation to student and classroom outcomes. *Review of Educational Research, 79*(1), 491–525.

Johnston, J. M., & Pennypacker, H. S. (1993). *Strategies and tactics of human behavioral research* (2nd ed.). Hillsdale, NJ: Lawrence Erlbaum Associates.

Jones, D. S., Podolsky, S. H., & Greene, J. A. (2012). The burden of disease and the changing task of medicine. *The New England Journal of Medicine, 366*(25), 2333–2338. doi: 10.1056/NEJMp1113569

Kantorski, B., Sanford-Dolly, C.W., Commisso, D. R., & Pollack, J. A. (2019). Backward design as a mobile application development strategy. *Educational Technology Research and Development, 67*(3), 711–731.

Katsiyannis, A., Yell, M., & Bradley, R. (2001). Reflections on the 25th anniversary of the Individuals with Disabilities Education Act. *Remedial and Special Education, 22*(6), 324–334.

Katz, I., & Assor, A. (2006). When choice motivates and when it does not. *Educational Psychology Review, 19*(4), 429–442. doi:10.1007/s10648-006-9027-y

Katz, J. (2013). The three-block model of universal design for learning (UDL): Engaging students in inclusive education. *Canadian Journal of Education, 36*(1), 153–194.

Kavale, K. A. (2010). Mainstreaming to full inclusion: From orthogenesis to pathogenesis of an idea. *International Journal of Disability, Development and Education, 49*(2), 201–214. doi:10.1080/103491220141776

Kay, S. (2016). *Postcards by Sarah Kay* (Poem #5). Accessed at https://nerdytalksbookblog .wordpress.com/2016/04/06/postcards-by-sarah-kay-poem4/ on April 27, 2020.

Kelly, J., & Pohl, B. (2018). Using structured positive and negative reinforcement to change student behavior in educational settings in order to achieve student academic success. *Multidisciplinary Journal for Education, Social and Technological Sciences, 5*(1), 17–29.

Kiefer, S. M., Alley, K. M., & Ellerbrock, C. R. (2015). Teacher and peer support for young adolescents' motivation, engagement, and school belonging. *Research in Middle Level Education, 38*(8), 1–18. doi:10.1080/19404476.2015.11641184

Killian, S. (2014). *10 evidence-based teaching strategies—The core list.* Accessed at http:// www.evidencebasedteaching.org.au/evidence-based-teaching-strategies/ on April 27, 2020.

Kos, J. M., Richdale, A. L., & Hay, D. A. (2006). Children with attention deficit hyperactivity disorder and their teachers: A review of the literature. *International Journal of Disability, Development and Education, 53*(2), 147–160. doi:10.1080/10349120600716125

Kosanovich, M., Weinstein, C., & Goldman, E. (2009). *Using student center activities to differentiate reading instruction: A guide for teachers.* Portsmouth, NH: RMC Research Corporation, Center on Instruction. Accessed at https://files.eric.ed.gov /fulltext/ED521607.pdf on April 27, 2020.

Kounin, J. S. (1970). *Discipline and group management in classrooms.* New York, NY: Holt, Rinehart & Winston.

Kunter, M., Baumert, J., & Köller, O. (2007). Effective classroom management and the development of subject-related interest. *Learning and Instruction, 17*(5), 494–509. doi:10.1016/j.learninstruc.2007.09.002

Landrum, T. J., & McDuffie, K. A. (2010). Learning styles in the age of differentiated instruction. *Exceptionality, 18*(1), 6–17. doi:10.1080/09362830903462441

Lauermann, F. (2014). Teacher responsibility from the teacher's perspective. *International Journal of Educational Research, 65,* 75–88.

Laursen, E. K. (2015). The power of grit, perseverance, and tenacity. *Reclaiming Children and Youth, 23*(4), 19–24.

Leahy, S., Lyon, C., Thompson, M., & Wiliam, D. (2005). Classroom assessment: Minute by minute, day by day. *Educational Leadership, 63*(3), 19–24.

Levy, E. (2007). *Gradual release of responsibility: I do, we do, you do.* Accessed at https://www.washoeschools.net/cms/lib/NV01912265/Centricity/Domain/257 /Certified%20Hiring/GradualReleaseResponsibilityJan08.pdf on April 27, 2020.

Levy, H. M. (2008). Meeting the needs of all students through differentiated instruction: Helping every child reach and exceed standards. *The Clearing House*, *81*(4), 161–164.

Lewis, P. J. (2016). Brain friendly teaching—reducing learner's cognitive load. *Academic Radiology*, *23*(7), 877–880.

Lindley, R. H. (1966). Recoding as a function of chunking and meaningfulness. *Psychonomic Science*, *6*(8), 393–394.

Little, C. (2020). Principles of behaviour support. In *Inclusive education in schools and early childhood settings* (pp. 93–101). Springer Singapore.

Liu, Z. X., Grady, C., & Moscovitch, M. (2018). The effect of prior knowledge on post-encoding brain connectivity and its relation to subsequent memory. *NeuroImage*, *167*, 211–223.

Long, M. H. (1980). Inside the "black box": Methodological issues in classroom research on language learning. *Language Learning*, *30*(1), 1–42.

Loughran, J. (2013). *Developing a pedagogy of teacher education: Understanding teaching and learning about teaching*. New York, NY: Routledge.

Maag, J. W. (2001). Rewarded by punishment: Reflections on the disuse of positive reinforcement in education. *Exceptional Children*, *67*(2), 173–186.

Maazouzi, K. (2017). Discipline problem in the classroom and its remedies. *London Journal of Research in Humanities and Social Sciences*, *17*(3), 63–73.

Mace, R. (1985). Universal design: Barrier-free environments for everyone. *Designers West*, *33*(1), 147–152.

Magner, L. (2000). Reaching all children through differentiated assessment: The 2-5-8 plan. *Gifted Child Today*, *23*(3), 48–50.

Mahvar, T., Farahani, M. A., & Aryankhesal, A. (2018). Conflict management strategies in coping with students' disruptive behaviors in the classroom: Systematized review. *Journal of Advances in Medical Education & Professionalism*, *6*(3), 102.

Mameli, C., Grazia, V., & Molinari, L. (2020). Agency, responsibility and equity in teacher versus student-centred school activities: A comparison between teachers' and learners' perceptions. *Journal of Educational Change*, pp. 1–17.

Marks, L. J., & Olson, J. C. (1981). Toward a cognitive structure conceptualization of product familiarity. *Advances in Consumer Research, North American Advances*, 8, 145–150.

Martella, R. C., Nelson, J. R., & Marchand-Martella, N. E. (2003). *Managing disruptive behaviors in the schools: A schoolwide, classroom, and individualized social learning approach*. Boston, MA: Allyn & Bacon.

Martin, A. J. (2013). Holding back and holding behind: Grade retention and students' non-academic and academic outcomes. *British Educational Research Journal*, *37*(5), 739–763. doi:10.1080/01411926.2010.490874

Martin, A. J., Linfoot, K., & Stephenson, J. (1999). How teachers respond to concerns about misbehavior in their classroom. *Psychology in the Schools*, *36*(4), 347–358.

Martin, E., Martin, R., & Terman, D. (1996). The legislative and litigation history of special education. *The Future of Children*, *6*(1), 25–39.

Martinez, A., Mcmahon, S. D., Coker, C., & Keys, C. B. (2016). Teacher behavioral practices: Relations to student risk behaviors, learning barriers, and school climate. *Psychology in the Schools*, *53*(8), 817–830.

Marzano Center. (2012). *Marzano design question 2: Helping students interact with new knowledge.* Accessed at https://blog.learningsciences.com/2016/01/05/helping-students-effectively-interact-with-new-knowledge-visual-instruction/ on July 14, 2020.

Marzano, R. J. (2007). *The art and science of teaching.* Alexandria, VA: Association for Supervision and Curriculum Development.

Marzano, R. J. (2009a). *Designing and teaching learning goals and objectives.* Bloomington, IN: Marzano Resources.

Marzano, R. J. (2009b). Setting the record straight on "high yield" strategies. *Phi Delta Kappan*, *91*(1), 30–37.

Marzano, R. J., & Brown, J. L. (2009). *Handbook for the art and science of teaching.* Alexandria, VA: Association for Supervision and Curriculum Development.

Marzano, R. J., & Marzano, J. S. (2001). The key to classroom management. *Educational Leadership*, *61*(1), 6–13.

Marzano, R. J., Marzano, J. S., & Pickering, D. J. (2003). *Classroom management that works.* Alexandria, VA: Association for Supervision and Curriculum Development.

Marzano, R. J., Pickering, D., & Pollock, J. E. (2001). *Classroom instruction that works: Research-based strategies for increasing student achievement.* Alexandria, VA: Association for Supervision and Curriculum Development.

Maslow, A. (1943). A theory of human motivation. *Psychological Review*, *50*, 370–390.

Mayzner, M. S., & Gabriel, R. F. (1963). Information "chunking" and short-term retention. *The Journal of Psychology*, *56*(1), 161–164.

McCoy, A. (2011). *Teaching new concepts: "I do it, we do it, you do it" method.* Accessed at http://antoinemccoy.com/teaching-new-concepts on April 24, 2020.

McDowell, M. (2020). *Teaching for transfer: A guide for designing learning with real-world application.* Bloomington, IN: Solution Tree.

McEvoy, A., & Welker, R. (2000). Antisocial behavior, academic failure, and school climate: A critical review. *Journal of Emotional and Behavioral Disorders*, *8*(3), 130–140. doi:10.1177/106342660000800301

McIntosh, K., Brown, J. A., & Borgmeier, C. J. (2008). Validity of functional behavior assessment within a response to intervention framework: Evidence, recommended practice, and future directions. *Assessment for Effective Intervention, 34*(1), 6–14. doi:10.1177/1534508408314096

McIntosh, R., Vaughn, S., Schumm, J., Haager, D., & Lee, O. (1994). Observations of students with learning disabilities in general education classrooms. *Exceptional Children, 60*(3), 249–261.

McTighe, J., & Brown, J. L. (2005). Differentiated instruction and educational standards: Is détente possible? *Theory Into Practice, 44*(3), 234–244. doi:10.1207 /s15430421tip4403_8

McTighe, J., & O'Connor, K. (2009). Seven practices for effective learning. In K. Ryan & J. M. Cooper (Eds.), *Kaleidoscope: Contemporary and classic readings in education* (pp. 174–180). Toronto, ON, Canada: Cengage Learning.

McTighe, J., & Wiggins, G. (1999). *The understanding by design handbook.* Alexandria, VA: Association for Supervision and Curriculum Development.

Meyer, A., Rose, D. H., & Gordon, D. (2016). *Universal design for learning: Theory and practice.* Wakefield, MA: CAST Professional.

Minarik, D. W., & Lintner, T. (2011). The push for inclusive classrooms and the impact on social studies design and delivery. *Social Studies Review, 50*(1), 52–55.

Moll, L. C. (1992). *Vygotsky and education: Instructional implications and applications of sociohistorical psychology.* Cambridge, UK: Cambridge University Press.

Mulyono, D., Asmawi, M., & Nuriah, T. (2018). The effect of reciprocal teaching, student facilitator and explaining and learning independence on mathematical learning results by controlling the initial ability of students. *International Electronic Journal of Mathematics Education, 13*(3), 199–205.

Murphy, J., & Hallinger, P. (2006). Equity as access to learning: Curricular and instructional treatment differences. *Journal of Curriculum Studies, 21*(2), 129–149. doi:10.1080/0022027890210203

Myers, D. G. (1999). *Exploring psychology* (4th ed.). New York, NY: Worth.

Nadelson, L. S., Throndsen, J., Campbell, J. E., Arp, M., Durfee, M., Dupree, K., et al. (2016). Are they using the data? Teacher perceptions of, practices with, and preparation to use assessment data. *International Journal of Education, 8*(3), 50–70.

Nicol, D. J., & Macfarlane-Dick, D. (2006). Formative assessment and self-regulated learning: A model and seven principles of good feedback practice. *Studies in Higher Education, 31*(2), 199–218.

Noble, T., & McGrath, H. (2008). The positive educational practices framework: A tool for facilitating the work of educational psychologists in promoting pupil wellbeing. *Educational & Child Psychology, 25*(2), 119–134.

Nussbaum, J. F. (1992). Effective teacher behaviors. *Communication Education*, *41*(2), 167–180. doi:10.1080/03634529209378878

Obi, Z. C. (2020). Classroom management for effective teaching and learning: The implication for teacher control techniques. *Nnadiebube Journal of Education*, *5*(2), 15–20.

O'Hara, S., & Pritchard, R. H. (2008). Meeting the challenge of diversity: Professional development for teacher educators. *Teacher Education Quarterly*, *35*(1), 43–61.

Ontario Ministry of Education. (2010). *Growing success: Assessment, evaluation, and reporting in Ontario schools*. Accessed at http://www.edu.gov.on.ca/eng /policyfunding/growSuccess.pdf on April 24, 2020.

Osborne, M. J. (2019). *The effects of reinforcement context on the effectiveness of social consequences* (Doctoral thesis, University of Waikato, Hamilton, New Zealand). Accessed at https://hdl.handle.net/10289/12550 on July 14, 2020.

OSEP Center on Positive Behavioral Interventions and Supports et al. (2000). Applying positive behavior support and functional behavioral assessment in schools. *Journal of Positive Behavior Interventions*, *2*(3), 131–143. doi:10.1177/109830070000200302

Oxford English Dictionary (n.d.). Ecosystem. Accessed at https://en.oxforddictionaries.com/ definition/ecosystem on April 27, 2020.

Palincsar, A. S. (1986). Metacognitive strategy instruction. *Exceptional Children*, *53*(2), 118–125.

Pea, R. D. (2004). The social and technological dimensions of scaffolding and related theoretical concepts for learning, education, and human activity. *The Journal of the Learning Sciences*, *13*(3), 423–451.

Pereira, J. K., & Smith-Adcock, S. (2011). Child-centered classroom management. *Action in Teacher Education*, *33*(3), 254–264. doi:10.1080/01626620.2011.592111

Perkins, D. N., Allen, R., & Hafner, J. (1983). Difficulties in everyday reasoning. In W. Maxwell (Ed.), *Thinking: The frontier expands* (pp. 177–189). Hillsdale, NJ: Lawrence Erlbaum Associates.

Perkins, D. N., & Blythe, T. (1994). Putting understanding up front. *Educational Leadership*, *51*(5), 4–7.

Perkins, D. N., Jay, E., & Tishman, S. (1993). Beyond abilities: A dispositional theory of thinking. *Merrill-Palmer Quarterly: Journal of Developmental Psychology*, *39*(1), 1–21.

Perkins, D. N., & Tishman, S. (2001). Dispositional aspects of intelligence. In J. M. Collins & S. Messick (Eds.), *Intelligence and personality: Bridging the gap in theory and measurement* (pp. 237–262). London, UK: Psychology Press.

Perkins, D. N., Tishman, S., Ritchhart, R., Donis, K., & Andrade, A. (2000). Intelligence in the wild: A dispositional view of intellectual traits. *Educational Psychology Review*, *12*(3), 269–293.

Peterson, E. R., Rubie-Davies, C. M., Elley-Brown, M. J., Widdowson, D. A., Dixon, R. S., & Irving, S. E. (2011). Who is to blame? Students, teachers and parents views on who is responsible for student achievement. *Research in Education*, *86*(1), 1–12.

Peterson, P. L., & Corneaux, M. A. (1987). Teachers' schemata for classroom events: The mental scaffolding of teachers' thinking during classroom instruction. *Teaching and Teacher Education*, *3*(4), 319–331. doi:10.1016/0742-051X(87)90024-2

Peterson, P. L., Marx, R. W., & Clark, C. M. (1978). Teacher planning, teacher behavior, and student achievement. *American Educational Research Journal*, *15*(3), 417–432. doi:10.3102/00028312015003417

Phillips, S. (2008). Are we holding back our students that possess the potential to excel? *Education*, *129*(1), 50–55.

Pikulski, J. J., & Chard, D. J. (2005). Fluency: Bridge between decoding and reading comprehension. *The Reading Teacher*, *58*(6), 510–519.

Pilten, G. (2016). The evaluation of effectiveness of reciprocal teaching strategies on comprehension of expository texts. *Journal of Education and Training Studies*, *4*(10), 232–247.

Polick, A. S., Cullen, K. L., & Buskist, W. (2010). How teaching makes a difference in students' lives. *APS Observer*, *23*(7). Accessed at https://www.psychologicalscience .org/observer/how-teaching-makes-a-difference-in-students-lives on April 24, 2020.

Porath, S. (2014). Talk less, listen more: Conferring in the reader's workshop. *The Reading Teacher*, *67*(8), 627–635. doi:10.1002/trtr.1266

Rasmussen, K. (1998). Setting a positive tone. *Education Update*, *40*(6). Alexandria, VA: Association for Supervision and Curriculum Development. Accessed at https:// www.ascd.org/publications/newsletters/education-update/sept98/vol40/num06 /Setting-a-Positive-Tone.aspx on July 14, 2020.

Reeve, J., Ryan, R., Deci, E. L., & Jang, H. (2008). Understanding and promoting autonomous self-regulation: A self-determination theory perspective. In D. H. Schunk & B. J. Zimmerman (Eds.), *Motivation and self-regulated learning: Theory, research, and applications* (pp. 223–244). Milton Park, UK: Taylor & Francis.

Reid, G. (2008). *Motivating learners in the classroom: Ideas and strategies.* Thousand Oaks, CA: SAGE.

Renzulli, J. S. (1977). *The interest-a-lyzer.* Mansfield Center, CT: Creative Learning Press.

Reynolds, M. C., Wang, M. C., & Walberg, H. J. (1987). The necessary restructuring of special and general education. *Exceptional Children*, *53*(5), 391–398. doi.org /10.1177/001440298705300501

Richards, J. C. (2013). Curriculum approaches in language teaching: Forward, central and backward design. *Rec Journal*, *44*(1), 5–33.

Riordan, R. (2010). *The red pyramid.* New York, NY: Disney-Hyperion.

Roche, A., & Clarke, D. M. (2014). Teachers holding back from telling: A key to student persistence on challenging tasks. *Australian Primary Mathematics Classroom, 19*(4), 3–8.

Rockwell, S. (2006). *You can't make me! From chaos to cooperation in the elementary classroom.* Thousand Oaks, CA: Corwin.

Rose, D. (2000). Universal design for learning. *Journal of Special Education Technology, 15*(4), 47–51.

Rose, D. H., & Meyer, A. (2002). *Teaching every student in the digital age: Universal design for learning.* Alexandria, VA: Association for Supervision and Curriculum Development.

Rose, D. H., & Meyer, A. (2006). *A practical reader in universal design for learning.* Cambridge, MA: Harvard Education Press.

Rosenshine, B. (2009). Systematic instruction. In T. L. Good (Ed.), *21st century education: A reference handbook* (Vol. 1). Thousand Oaks, CA: SAGE.

Rowe, M. B. (1986). Wait time: Slowing down may be a way of speeding up! *Journal of Teacher Education, 37*(1), 43–50. doi:10.1177/002248718603700110

Rueda, R., Gallego, M. A., & Moll, L. C. (2000). The least restrictive environment: A place or a context? *Remedial and Special Education, 21*(2), 70–78. doi:10.1177/074193250002100202

Rutherford, P. (2008). *Instruction for all students.* Alexandria, VA: Just Ask.

Ryan, R. M., & Deci, E. L. (2000). Self-determination theory and the facilitation of intrinsic motivation, social development, and wellbeing. *American Psychologist, 55*(1), 68–78. doi:10.1037/0003-066X.55.1.68

Sadler, D. R. (1989). Formative assessment and the design of instructional systems. *Instructional Science, 18*, 119–144.

Salend, S. J., & Garrick Duhaney, L. M. (2011). Historical and philosophical changes in the education of students with exceptionalities. In A. F. Rotatori, F. E. Obiakor, & J. P. Bakken (Eds.), *Advances in special education: History of special education* (Vol. 21, pp. 1–20). Bingley, UK: Emerald.

Saphier, J., & Gower, R. (1997). *The skillful teacher: Building your teaching skills.* Acton, MA: Research for Better Teaching.

Savery, J. R. (2015). Overview of problem-based learning: Definitions and distinctions. *Essential Readings in Problem-Based Learning: Exploring and Extending the Legacy of Howard S. Barrows, 9*, 5–15.

Schmidt, J. J. (1982). Understanding punishment and encouraging positive discipline. *Journal of Humanistic Education and Development, 21*(1), 43–48.

Schunk, D. H., Meece, J. L., & Pintrich, P. R. (2008). *Motivation in education: Theory, research, and applications* (3rd ed.). New York, NY: Pearson.

Schwan, S., & Riempp, R. (2004). The cognitive benefits of interactive videos: Learning to tie nautical knots. *Learning and Instruction*, *14*(3), 293–305.

Scruggs, T. E., & Mastropieri, M. A. (1996). Teacher perceptions of mainstreaming /inclusion, 1958–1995: A research synthesis. *Exceptional Children*, *63*(1), 59–74.

Segers, M., & Dochy, F. (2006). Introduction: Enhancing student learning through assessment: Alignment between levels of assessment and different effects on learning. *Studies in Educational Evaluation*, *32*(3), 171–179.

Seidel, T., Rimmele, R., & Prenzel, M. (2005). Clarity and coherence of lesson goals as a scaffold for student learning. *Learning and Instruction*, *15*(6), 539–556.

Seifert, T. (2004). Understanding student motivation. *Educational Research*, *46*(2), 137–149.

Shepard, L. A. (2000). The role of assessment in a learning culture. *Educational Research*, *29*(7), 4–14.

Shores, R. E., Jack, S. L., Gunter, P. L., Ellis, D. N., DeBriere, T. J., & Wehby, J. H. (1993). Classroom interactions of children with behavior disorders. *Journal of Emotional and Behavioral Disorders*, *1*(1), 27–39. doi:10.1177/106342669300100106

Shults, K., Brock, C., Millay, K., & Keesey, S. (2019). *Is the punishment worth it?* [Poster session]. Posters at the Capitol, Kentucky.

Sieberer-Nagler, K. (2016). Effective classroom-management & positive teaching. *English Language Teaching*, *9*(1), 163–172.

Simpkins, P. M., Mastropieri, M. A., & Scruggs, T. E. (2009). Differentiated curriculum enhancements in inclusive fifth-grade science classes. *Remedial and Special Education*, *30*(5), 300–308.

Simpson, M. (1997). Developing differentiation practices: Meeting the needs of pupils and teachers. *The Curriculum Journal*, *8*(1), 85–104.

Sizer, T. R., & Sizer, N. F. (2000). *The students are watching: Schools and the moral contract.* Boston, MA: Beacon Press.

Skiba, R. J., & Rausch, M. K. (2013). Zero tolerance, suspension, and expulsion: Questions of equity and effectiveness. In C. M. Evertson & C. S. Weinstein (Eds.), *Handbook of classroom management* (pp. 1063–1089). New York, NY: Taylor & Francis.

Smith, M., & Smith, K. E. (2000). "I believe in inclusion but . . .": Regular education early children teachers' perceptions of successful inclusion. *Journal of Research in Childhood Education*, *142*(2), 161–180.

Squire, L. R. (1992). "Memory and the hippocampus: A synthesis from findings with rats, monkeys, and humans": Correction. *Psychological Review*, *99*(3), 582. Accessed at https://doi.org/10.1037/0033-295X.99.3.582 on July 14, 2020.

Snyder, D. (1953). A brief history of differentiated instruction. *My Back Pages*, *4*(425). Accessed at http://www.ascd.org/ascd-express/vol4/425-mybackpages.aspx on April 21, 2020.

Soleman, M. A. E. M., Ata, O. A., & Salah, H. A. (2019). Gentle teaching: Foundations and strategies in reducing reading disabilities. *SVU-Journal of Abstracts*, *1*(1), 22.

Sousa, D. A. (2006). *How the brain learns* (3rd ed.). Thousand Oaks, CA: Corwin.

Sousa, D. A. (2016). *How the brain learns* (5th ed.). Thousand Oaks, CA: Corwin.

Spearman, C. (1904). "General intelligence" objectively determined and measured. *The American Journal of Psychology*, *15*(2), 201–292.

Spilt, J. L., Leflot, G., Onghena, P., & Colpin, H. (2016). Use of praise and reprimands as critical ingredients of teacher behavior management: Effects on children's development in the context of a teacher-mediated classroom intervention. *Prevention Science*, *17*(6), 732–742. doi:10.1007/s11121-016-0667-y

Stanford, B., & Reeves, S. (2009). Making it happen: Using differentiated instruction, retrofit framework, and universal design for learning. *Teaching Exceptional Children Plus*, *5*(6), 1–9.

Stiggins, R., & DuFour, R. (2009). Maximizing the power of formative assessments. *Phi Delta Kappan*, *90*(9), 640–644.

Strangman, N., Vue, G., Hall, T., & Meyer, A. (2003). *Graphic organizers and implications for universal design for learning: Curriculum enhancement report.* Wakefield, MA: National Center on Accessing the General Curriculum.

Stronge, J. H., & Tucker, P. D. (2000). *Teacher evaluation and student achievement.* Washington, DC: National Education Association.

Struyven, K., Dochy, F., & Janssens, S. (2005). Students' perceptions about evaluation and assessment in higher education: A review. *Assessment and Evaluation in Higher Education*, *30*(4), 325–341.

Sutton, R. E., Mudrey-Camino, R., & Knight, C. C. (2009). Teachers' emotion regulation and classroom management. *Theory Into Practice*, *48*(2), 130–137. doi:10.1080/00405840902776418

Swanson, H. L. (2001). Searching for the best model for instructing students with learning disabilities. *Focus on Exceptional Children*, *34*(2), 1–14.

Sweller, J. (1994). Cognitive load theory, learning difficulty, and instructional design. *Learning and Instruction*, *4*(4), 295–312.

Sweller, J. (2011). Cognitive load theory. *Psychology of Learning and Motivation*, *55*, 37–76.

Tattoo, M. T. (1996). Examining values and beliefs about teaching diverse students: Understanding the challenges for teacher education. *Educational Evaluation and Policy Analysis*, *18*(2), 155–180. doi:10.3102/01623737018002155

Tauber, R. T. (1995). *Classroom management: Sound theory and effective practice* (4th ed.). Westport, CT: Praeger.

Theodore Roosevelt Center. (n.d.). *Theodore Roosevelt quotes.* Accessed at http://www .theodorerooseveltcenter.org/Learn-About-TR/TR-Quotes?page=3 on April 21, 2020.

Tomlinson, C. A. (1999). *The differentiated classroom: Responding to the needs of all learners.* Alexandria, VA: Association for Supervision and Curriculum Development.

Tomlinson, C. (2001). *How to differentiate instruction in mixed ability classrooms* (2nd ed.). Alexandria, VA: Association for Supervision and Curriculum Development.

Tomlinson, C. A. (2003). *Fulfilling the promise of the differentiated classroom: Strategies and tools for responsive teaching.* Alexandria, VA: Association for Supervision and Curriculum Development.

Tomlinson, C. A. (2009). Learning profiles and achievement. *School Administrator, 66*(2), 28–34.

Tomlinson, C. A. (2014). *The differentiated classroom: Responding to the needs of all learners* (2nd ed.). Alexandria, VA: Association for Supervision and Curriculum Development.

Tomlinson, C. A., Brighton, C., Hertberg, H., Callahan, C. M., Moon, T. R., Brimijoin, K., et al. (2003). Differentiating instruction in response to student readiness, interest, and learning profile in academically diverse classrooms: A review of literature. *Journal for the Education of the Gifted, 27*(2/3), 119–145.

Tomlinson, C. A., & Imbeau, M. B. (2014). *A differentiated approach to the Common Core: How do I help a broad range of learners succeed with challenging curriculum?* Alexandria, VA: Association for Supervision and Curriculum Development.

Tomlinson, C. A., & McTighe, J. (2006). *Integrating differentiated instruction and understanding by design: Connecting content and kids.* Alexandria, VA: Association for Supervision and Curriculum Development.

Tomlinson, C. A., & Moon, T. R. (2013). *Assessment and student success in a differentiated classroom.* Alexandria, VA: Association for Supervision and Curriculum Development.

Tonelson, S. W. (1981). The importance of teacher self-concept to create a healthy psychological environment for learning. *Education, 102*(1), 96–100.

Trussell, R. P. (2008). Classroom universals to prevent problem behaviors. *Intervention in School and Clinic, 43*(3), 179–185. doi: 10.1177/1053451207311678

Tse, D., Langston, R. F., Kakeyama, M., Bethus, I., Spooner, P. A., Wood, E. R., et al. (2007). Schemas and memory consolidation. *Science, 316*(5821), 76–82.

U.S. Department of Education. (1975). *Public Law 94-142: 94th Congress* [89 STAT. 773]. Washington, DC: Government Publishing Office.

U.S. Department of Education. (2010). *Thirty-five years of progress in educating children with disabilities through IDEA*. Accessed at www2.ed.gov/about/offices/list/osers /idea35/history/idea-35-history.pdf on April 24, 2020.

Umbreit, J. (1996). Functional analysis of disruptive behavior in an inclusive classroom. *Journal of Early Intervention, 20*(1), 18–29.

University of Kansas. (n.d). *Tiered assignments*. Accessed at www.specialconnections.ku .edu/?q=instruction/universal_design_for_learning/teacher_tools/tiered_assignments on April 24, 2020.

Urdan, T., & Schoenfelder, E. (2006). Classroom effects on student motivation: Goal structures, social relationships, and competence beliefs. *Journal of School Psychology, 44*(5), 331–349. doi:10.1016/j.jsp.2006.04.003

van de Pol, J., Volman, M., & Beishuizen, J. (2010). Scaffolding in teacher-student interaction: A decade of research. *Educational Psychology Review, 22*(3), 271–296. doi:10.1007/s10648-010-9127-6

van Kesteren, M. T. R., Krabbendam, L., & Meeter, M. (2018). Integrating educational knowledge: Reactivation of prior knowledge during educational learning enhances memory integration. *NPJ Science of Learning, 3*(1), 1–8.

VanLehn, K. (1988). Student modeling. In M. C. Polson & J. J. Richardson (Eds.), *Foundations of intelligent tutoring systems* (pp. 55–78). Hillsdale, NJ: Lawrence Erlbaum Associates.

van Merriënboer, J. J. G., & Ayres, P. (2005). Research on cognitive load theory and its design implications for e-learning. *Educational Technology Research and Development, 53*(3), 5–13.

van Merriënboer, J. J. G., & Sweller, J. (2005). Cognitive load theory and complex learning: Recent developments and future directions. *Educational Psychology Review, 17*(2), 147–177.

Volante, L., & Beckett, D. (2011). Formative assessment and the contemporary classroom: Synergies and tensions between research and practice. *Canadian Journal of Education, 34*(2), 239–255.

Vygotsky, L. S. (1978). *Mind in society: The development of higher psychological processes*. Cambridge, MA: Harvard University Press.

Washburne, C. W. (1953). Adjusting the program to the child. *Educational Leadership, 11*(3), 138–147.

Watts-Taffe, S., Laster, B. P., Broach, L., Marinak, B., McDonald Connor, C., & Walker-Dalhouse, D. (2012). Differentiated instruction: Making informed teacher decisions. *The Reading Teacher, 66*(4), 303–314.

Weber, C. (2018). *Behavior: The forgotten curriculum—An RTI approach for nurturing essential life skills*. Bloomington, IN: Solution Tree Press.

Weiner, B. (1972). Attribution theory, achievement motivation, and the educational process. *Review of Educational Research, 42*(2), 203–215.

Welch, A. B. (2000). Responding to student concerns about fairness. *Teaching Exceptional Children, 33*(2), 36–40.

Westwood, P. (2016). *What teachers need to know about differentiated instruction.* Melbourne, Australia: Australian Council for Educational Research.

Whetten, D. A. (2007). Principles of effective course design: What I wish I had known about learning-centered teaching 30 years ago. *Journal of Management Education, 31*(3), 339–357. doi:10.1177/1052562906298445

Wiggins, G. (1990). *The case for authentic assessment.* Accessed at https://files.eric.ed.gov /fulltext/ED328611.pdf on April 24, 2020.

Wiggins, G. (1998). *Educative assessment: Designing assessments to inform and improve student performance.* San Francisco, CA: Jossey-Bass.

Wiggins, G., & McTighe, J. (1998). *Understanding by Design.* Alexandria, VA: Association for Supervision and Curriculum Development.

Wiggins, G., & McTighe, J. (2007). *Schooling by Design: Mission, action, and achievement.* Alexandria, VA: Association for Supervision and Curriculum Development.

Wiggins, G., & McTighe, J. (2011). *The Understanding by Design guide to creating high-quality units.* Alexandria, VA: Association for Supervision and Curriculum Development.

Wiliam, D. (2009). *Assessment for learning: Why, what and how?* London, UK: Institute of Education, University of London.

Wiliam, D. (2014). *Formative assessment and contingency in the regulation of learning processes.* Accessed at https://famemichigan.org/wp-content /uploads/2018/06/Wiliam-Formative-assessment-and-contingency-in -the-regulation-of-learning-processes.pdf on April 24, 2020.

Wiliam, D. (2017). *Embedded formative assessment* (2nd ed.). Bloomington, IN: Solution Tree Press.

Willis, J. (2007). Review of research: Brain-based teaching strategies for improving students' memory, learning, and test-taking success. *Childhood Education, 83*(5), 310–315.

Wilson, G. L. (2016). Revisiting classroom routines. *Educational Leadership, 73*(4), 50–55.

Wolff, C. E., Jarodzka, H., van den Bogert, N., & Boshuizen, H. P. (2016). Teacher vision: expert and novice teachers' perception of problematic classroom management scenes. *Instructional Science, 44*(3), 243–265.

Wolff, C. E., Jarodzka, H., & Boshuizen, H. P. (2017). See and tell: Differences between expert and novice teachers' interpretations of problematic classroom management events. *Teaching and Teacher Education, 66,* 295–308.

Wood, C. (2002). Changing the pace of school: Slowing down the day to improve the quality of learning. *Phi Delta Kappan, 83*(7), 545–550.

Yahaya, A. (2014). *Abraham Maslow: The needs hierarchy.* Accessed at http://eprints.utm .my/id/eprint/6091/1/aziziyahbrahamMaslow.pdf on July 18, 2015.

Yeager, D. S., & Dweck, C. S. (2012). Mindsets that promote resilience: When students believe that personal characteristics can be developed. *Educational Psychologist, 47*(4), 302–314.

Zarrabi, F. (2017). How explicit listening strategy instruction affects listening comprehension of different learners. *Journal of Language Teaching and Research, 8*(4), 655–662.

Zimmerman, B. J. (1989). A social cognitive view of self-regulated academic learning. *Journal of Educational Psychology, 81*(3), 329–339. doi:10.1037/00220663.81.3.329

Zimmerman, B. J. (2002). Becoming a self-regulated learner: An overview. *Theory Into Practice, 41*(2), 64–70.

Zimmerman, B. J. (2013). Theories of self-regulated learning and academic achievement: An overview and analysis. In B. J. Zimmerman & D. H. Schunk (Eds.), *Self-regulated learning and academic achievement: Theory, research, and practice* (pp. 10–45). Abingdon, UK: Routledge.

INDEX

A

ability
   defined, 155–156
addressing avoidance behaviors, 70, 74
altering triggers, 70, 72–73, 88
anchor activities, 49, 63
   defined, 127
   differentiated instruction, 120, 127–128, 132
   history, 131
   language arts, 128–129
   mathematics, 130–131
   music, 131
   science, 131
   template, 149
Anderson, L., 133, 141
antecedents. *See* triggers
appreciating all students, 10, 14, 21
assessment, 15
   developing an instrument, 96, 99
   formative, 5–6, 32, 89–108, 168
   preassessment, 48–49, 63, 71
   summative, 37, 90
attention deficit hyperactivity disorder (ADHD), 77
   differentiated instruction, 119

attention seeking
   diverting, 70, 75–77
attribute theory
   to understand perseverance, 152
   cases, 153
automaticity. *See* consolidation and automaticity
autonomy
   professional, 168
   teaching, 158, 160, 163, 165
avoidance, 69–70
   addressing, 70, 74
avoiding overstimulation, 72
avoiding reinforcement, 7, 72–73

B

backward design, 26
being prepared. *See* preparedness
Berry, R., 116
Black and Wiliam's formative assessment theory, 91–93
Black, P., 93, 95
Bloom's revised taxonomy, 61, 133, 140
bottom–up approach, 46

C

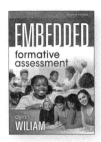

Embedded Formative Assessment, Second Edition
Dylan Wiliam

The second edition of this best-selling resource presents new research, insights, examples, and formative assessment techniques teachers can immediately apply in their classrooms. Updated examples and templates help teachers elicit evidence of learning, provide meaningful feedback, and empower students to take ownership of their education.

BKF790

Inclusion Strategies and Interventions, Second Edition
Toby J. Karten

In inclusive classrooms, students with special educational needs are treated as integral members of the general education environment. Gain strategies to offer the academic, social, emotional, and behavioral benefits that allow all students to achieve their highest potential.

BKF381

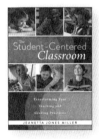

The Student-Centered Classroom
Jeanetta Jones Miller

Student-centered classrooms allow schools to fulfill their most enduring promise: to give students a fair chance to grow up literate, open-minded, and prepared to succeed. Begin making this critically important shift in your classroom with this resource as your guide.

BKF951

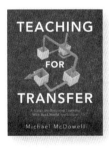

Teaching for Transfer
Michael McDowell

Empower students to become creative, well-rounded citizens, prepared to meet and overcome real-world challenges. With *Teaching for Transfer*, you will discover a road map for reconfiguring K–12 classroom instruction to ensure learners can expertly apply their knowledge and skills to new contexts.

BKF950

GL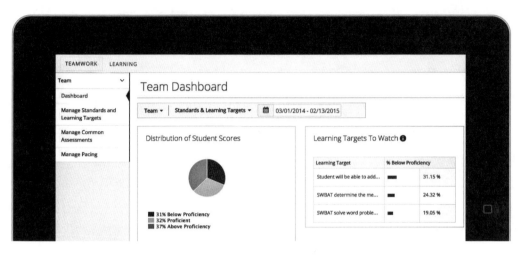BAL **PD**

The **Power to Improve**
Is in Your Hands

Global PD gives educators focused and goals-oriented training from top experts. You can rely on this innovative online tool to improve instruction in every classroom.

- Get unlimited, on-demand access to guided video and book content from top Solution Tree authors.

- Improve practices with personalized virtual coaching from PLC-certified trainers.

- Customize learning based on skill level and time commitments.